Claiming A Frontier:

MINISTRY

AND

OLDER PEOPLE

ROBERT W. McCLELLAN

This Monograph is published by the
Ethel Percy Andrus Gerontology Center
University of Southern California

RICHARD H. DAVIS, Ph.D.
Director of Publications and Media Projects

First Printing 1977
Second Printing 1979

THE UNIVERSITY OF SOUTHERN CALIFORNIA PRESS

ISBN 0-88474-040-4

Library of Congress Catalog Card Number 77-085413

Book Design: Richard Bohen
Cover Artist: Jesus Perez
Illustrator: Kim Rarig

To the Author of Life,
and to all who in that Name
shared in making and distributing this book;
especially members and friends of
Chatsworth Adult Center,
Point Loma Community Presbyterian Church,
San Diego, California

Foreword

This book makes a major contribution to a field of gerontology which has been abysmally neglected. Although no field of research or social practice has burgeoned so much as that of the study of aging in the past two decades, very little experimental or theoretical work has been done on the relation of church practices to successful aging. It is consequently delightful to herald the appearance of this unique and helpful book. It ought to have a mighty impact on churches whose congregations are in the main aging and older. It is unique in that it presents the results of a series of experiments that have been field tested and evaluated. It is helpful because it flows out of the stream of actual church experience.

It is always interesting and significant to trace the origins of social innovation. I have been involved in the growth of the experience reported in this book from the beginning. Dr. Kenneth P. Berg, chairman of the board of Christian Services Inc. — a non-profit corporation supervising fifty retirement villages stressing life care across the nation — asked me to supervise the D. Min. on which he was working at the San Francisco Theological Seminary. His wealth of experience led him to propound twelve techniques which he felt might revitalize church life through a vital ministry to the aged. His twelve concepts were the product of his long experience with the aged, but they were speculative. Robert W. McClellan, the author of this book sensed their merit but felt that those theoretical statements ought to be operationalized, tested, and established in practice. Dr. McClellan's D. Min. work consisted of that effort. He cherished the background work of Dr. Berg, but he refined those theoretical concepts as the result of his field operations in the Pt. Loma Community Presbyterian Church, San Diego, California. What is presented in this book is thus a product of two innovative minds working through common themes but in different ways. This final result has the value of a rich number of creative designs by which every church may begin to serve their aging members.

This work is but one of a number of very recent approaches to aging by church groups. Attention should be given to the Catholic program called Project: HEAD that came out of experience of Catholic groups in Philadelphia. Some focus should be centered on The Shepherd's Center concept which came out of the work done in a consortium of churches in Kansas City, Missouri, and which has now been repeated in Atlanta, Georgia. The Interfaith Coalition of Aging joining together one hundred million members of Jewish, Catholic, and Protestant churches is stimulating interest and programmatic efforts by synagogues and churches across the nation. The vast potential of religious groups for the elderly is beginning to be realized and it is long past time that such promise should be vitalized. This book brings together much of all that is promising in all of these programs.

There is an aspect of religion that is always ritualistic and dramatic. One of the serendipitous products of this program is the birth of that great character, *Samantha Muffin,* our winsome and dramatic mouse. If the only immortal product of this program was Samantha Muffin, all the effort of the program would have been justified. She is making and will continue to make inspirational visits across the nation. But there is far more. Any board of church or synagogue officers that reviews this book will find much that is relevant to growing programs for the aging in their institutions. In fact, many other types of institutions will do well to consider the recommendations that come from the experience of Dr. McClellan and his group of older persons.

James A. Peterson, Ph.D.
Andrus Gerontology Center
University of Southern California

Preface

This book is written by a pastor of the United Presbyterian Church with thirty-one years experience in large and small churches in both the eastern and western parts of America. His orientation and commitment is to the Christian faith and life with the person of Jesus Christ, the Lord of life, as central. His colleagues in the Christian ministry, and those in the Jewish community are the intended readers and users. Others are most welcome and may be interested and even helped in coming to grips with the field of aging as an area of academic, social and professional concern.

The origin of *Claiming a Frontier: Ministry and Older People* was in doctoral study related to the renewal and fulfillment of older persons, undertaken at San Francisco Theological Seminary, San Anselmo, California, and in conjunction with Dr. James A. Peterson, Ethel Percy Andrus Gerontology Center, University of Southern California, Los Angeles, California. A comprehensive record may be found in the writer's Dissertation/Project: "A Study of the Need and Possibilities for Renewal and Fulfillment of Older People in Church, Synagogue and Community" (San Francisco Theological Seminary, 1976).

Deep appreciation is expressed to all who have offered information, guidance and support for this work. Special thanks is given to thesis advisor, James A. Peterson, Ph.D.; editor Richard H. Davis, Ph.D.; assistant editor, Richard Bohen; friend and neighbor, Warren R. Baller, Ph.D., Professor of Psychology, United States International University, San Diego, California; members and leaders of Chatsworth Adult Center, San Diego, California; and most especially to Millie Lou McClellan, the writer's wife who lived both with the author and the book while truly sharing in active ministry among older people.

Robert W. McClellan, D.Min.

Contents

1   Still A Frontier

Everything ages. All that God has made is aging. All that man makes is aging. But only the human species is conscious of the aging process. The experience of aging is no respecter of persons. It happens to everyone. Whatever the racial origin, skin color, family background, social or financial status, or religious belief and practice, aging is real. We are together in the aging boat. We have much to share and much to learn about this God-intended process going on in and around us. We may seek to deny its reality, and to resist its ravages, or we may explore its possibilities.

The opportunities for participation in improving the lot of the aging through the ministry of congregations of churches and synagogues are only beginning to be perceived. Since congregations are the place of religious life and the "home" of pastors, priests and rabbis, we who are the leaders of congregations have a special privilege and responsibility to this segment of our people.

The traditional approach to older persons, both in secular and religious sectors, has been the effort to do something *to* and *for* them. The resulting message is clear. Seniors can only receive what others give. Their usefulness, if

1

any, is in employing the time, interest, and energy of others. Such an approach is unrewarding to the givers and degrading to the recipients. Often there is hostility, open or veiled, both in those who resent the drain on their resources, and in those who are treated as consumers of the benefactions of younger persons.

Fortunately there are new developments in gerontology (the science of aging) which provide a better foundation for the consideration of effective ministry among the aging and the aged. We are discovering several basic concerns.

Ministry *to* older persons will remain as an important aspect for individuals who need services offered to them, from pastoral care to community services.

Ministry *for* older persons will also continue because, collectively, they have special needs which they cannot meet themselves. Care must be taken, however, that ministries not be done for older persons to meet needs which they can handle themselves.

Ministry *with* the aging is emerging as the church/synagogue seeks to involve them as valid full partners in its ongoing total mission. The sense of belonging and fellowship calls forth creative effort and a feeling of well-being when older persons are included in planning and leading in ministry, especially in inter-generational settings.

Ministry *of* the aging occurs as the special gifts of maturity and experience of older persons are recognized, utilized, and appreciated in the church/synagogue and community. Some believe, the author included, this is the most basic and promising of all aspects of ministry *and* the aging because it enables older persons to remain in, or to re-enter the mainstream of involvement and service. They can use their time, energy, imagination, experience, concern, love, and money for persons and causes they want to support.

Added together, these make the aging and the aged a distinctive but not separated group. They are seen and known as an integral part of the whole congregational family, both receiving and giving in common with all other members of the family.

As spiritual leaders, while ours is the call to ultimates, and thus to the renewal and fulfillment of life, many of us feel that because of lack of time, experience, or other reasons (perhaps multiple) we have been unready, unwilling or ineffective in ministry among older persons.

Evidence shows such ministry has had a low priority; and all too often it has been dull, ineffective, and therefore, unrewarding to older persons, congregations, and communities. In spite of this, ministry among older persons may become one of the most challenging and rewarding experiences of church, synagogue and community leaders, both professional and volunteer!

In a very real way, neither our society nor our religious institutions, have been prepared for what is taking place in and around us. Older people are not new in human history. What is new is the lengthening of the life span and the rapidly increasing numbers of older persons. It has been shown that the farther back we go in human society, the earlier people become "old." The late Paul Dudley White, M.D., found in researching records of medical diagnoses at Massachusetts General Hospital fifty years ago, that one woman who had died at age forty-five in the late 1800s had only one diagnosis on her record: old age! (1973)

Again, the changing of roles of older persons in our culture has confused and deeply affected us. In most primitive societies the aged were held in great veneration and respect. Their hardiness enabled them to survive, and while there were few of them, they were the chief tribal sources of knowledge and information. Often they held positions of leadership. How in contrast is the remark an attractive fifty-five year old woman made to her pastor: "We just don't forgive people for getting old!"

As we approach this complex and often perplexing issue, three principles should be kept in mind while reading and using this book.

1. A New Frontier for the Church/Synagogue

In 1949 Paul B. Maves and Lennart J. Cedarleaf published the first comprehensive attempt to study the relationship of the Protestant churches to people over sixty years of age. In their work, *Older People and the*

Church, they described aging as "a new frontier for the Church." (Maves and Cedarleaf, 1949). Even though many churches and synagogues have ministries among older persons (some for a considerable period of time), the religious sector has been slow (except for pastoral ministry, hospitals and retirement homes) to enter into creative ministry among older persons.

2. **Leadership**
   The issue of leadership is of primary importance. No program can begin usefully, or remain effective, without good leadership. On the other hand, a pastor, priest, rabbi, social worker, or other specialist is not required, although each could be useful. What is needed is at least one person who loves people, sees the need, wants to help, is willing to learn, is flexible, patient and persistent, and has some group skills.

3. **Developmental Factors**
   Every situation is unique and invites a different approach. Among the factors to be considered are: size of congregation and community, numbers of older persons in the constituency, needs of older persons in church/synagogue and community, programs and resources available to meet needs of older persons in the church(es)/synagogue(s) and community.

A PROMISING FRONTIER

The frontier image still appeals to Americans. We are proud of our heritage. We look for frontiers even though we may believe all have been explored, exploited, or exhausted. Aging and the aged is becoming known as a great social and spiritual frontier. The fact is, ministry and older people is an expanding, urgent and promising frontier which is only beginning to be claimed by the religious sector. It calls for our attention and action. Thus, I have chosen the concept of a continuing frontier for the framework of this book. In support of this premise information is offered from three sources:

1. Updating his earlier (1949) concern for the "new frontier," Maves reported in 1960:

It cannot be determined at this time how extensive or how intense these local parish programs for older persons are. It is the writer's impression that, while some churches are rendering significant service to older persons, the vast majority of them still have made little effort to develop special programs or to lay increased emphasis upon the problems of aging. In this respect it is highly probable that the churches are neither far ahead nor far behind most other institutions in the community in the consciousness of and concern for the aged. (p. 723)

2. The National Interfaith Coalition on Aging, Inc., which grew out of the 1971 White House Conference on Aging, has become the single most inclusive ecumenical organization (Protestant, Catholic, Jewish, Orthodox) on a national basis, organized and committed to working in behalf of the aging and the aged. In a major study completed in 1976, *The Religious Sector Explores Its Mission in Aging: A Report on the Survey of Programs for the Aging under Religious Auspices (Cook),* the purpose of the project was:

To survey, catalogue, enlist and develop information related to resources and commitment of the religious sector for its action and participation in the follow-through of the White House Conference on Aging recommendations. (p. 22)

The survey was undertaken because no previous comprehensive study had been made by the religious sector related to programs specifically concerning aging and the aged, and only a paucity of data was available on this subject.

Begun in 1972 and completed in 1976, the survey brought responses from 111 national religious bodies, reporting on fifty-two categories of services in the area of aging on national, regional, area and local levels. The project resulted in the development of a first cycle data base in an electronic data-processing bank for use of the religious sector's follow-through in the White House Conference on Aging recommendations.

Out of a number of findings, one statement sums up a central conclusion:

Based upon the data examined in this report and inspection of program descriptions in the NICA data bank, it is the

opinion of the present investigator that, taken as a whole,
at present, religious bodies in the United States exhibit a
relatively low effort on behalf of the elderly. (p. 94)

3. My perspectives and convictions substantiate the above
   findings, and grew out of a study which included:
   a. A review of more than 200 pieces of literature related
      to sociological, psychological, Biblical and theological
      aspects of aging;
   b. A survey of pastors of Churches in the Presbytery of
      San Diego, United Presbyterian Church in the U.S.A.;
   c. Attendance at, and/or participation in thirteen meet-
      ings, retreats, workshops, and conferences related to
      aging; ranging in size and scope from small to large,
      and in sponsorship from local to national;
   d. Interview with fifty persons, most of whom are
      significant in secular and religious aspects of aging;
   e. A ten-month action/investigation project of the
      Chatsworth Adult Center, Point Loma Community
      Presbyterian Church, San Diego, California;
   f. Discovery, selection and evaluation of ecumenical
      models of programs which show evidence of renewal
      and fulfillment of older persons.

4. In spite of the high calling of spiritual well-being for
   older persons laid upon us, and the urgent need for attention to this summons, the findings of the study showed:
   a. There are few known comprehensive models of
      programs conducted by individual congregations or
      groups of congregations on a local basis which show
      evidence of renewal and fulfillment of older persons.
   b. It appears that most pastors, priests and rabbis are too
      busy or are not equipped; leadership in their
      congregations is unaware and unprepared, and older
      persons themselves are largely uninvolved in develop-
      ing programs for the renewal and fulfillment of older
      persons, even though the numbers and needs of older
      persons is great and growing.
   c. Older persons have unique problems which require
      more thoughtful, consistent attention than they are
      receiving from any sector of society. The church/
      synagogue has tended to follow rather than lead. The

fact that there is no comprehensive written theology of aging is a clear sign of the lack of adequate attention to the needs and possibilities of older persons from the Judeo-Christian point of view.

d. The experience of self-fulfillment in older persons leads to profound benefit to them and their congregations. With it, aging becomes more rewarding.

This book is a response to these realities. Its purpose is to offer a practical guide for ministry and older persons in the church, synagogue and community. The intention is to: 1. provide information; 2. encourage interest; 3. enable ministries; and 4. supply resources for readers to enter into, or improve their ministries in this field.

Thus, perhaps, will the final conclusion of the NICA study be set further forward:

> Whether one approaches the issue of religion and aging from the national level through the various religious bodies to the local church or synagogue or vice versa, what emerges is quite clear. The aging person in the United States of America is now to some extent reaping the rewards of an awakened religious community, and will undoubtedly in the future reap these rewards to an even greater extent. By fulfilling its spiritual mandate to love God and one's fellow man, the religious community at all levels will add the caring love and dignity which make life at all ages beautiful and meaningful. (Cook pp. 130-131)

Until then, ministry and older people is still a frontier!

REFERENCES

Cook, Thomas C. Jr. *The Religious Sector Explores its Mission in Aging: A Report on the Survey of Programs for the Aging under Religious Auspices.* National Interfaith Coalition on Aging, Athens, Georgia 1976.

Maves, Paul B. "Aging, Religion and the Church," in Tibbitts, C., *Handbook of Social Gerontology.* Chicago: Chicago University Press, 1960.

Maves, Paul B. and Cedarleaf, J. Lennart *Older People and the Church* New York: Abingdon-Cokesbury Press, 1949.

White, Paul Dudley, "Outgrowing Middle Age," in Pfeiffer, Eric (ed.), *Successful Aging,* Duke University: Center for Aging, 1974.

2 Scouting Out The Land

How shall we explain the dogged reluctance of the religious community to claim the frontier of ministry and the aging? One possible answer is "gerontophobia" (fear of aging), the name given to a prevalent fact in our culture. Yes, ours is a society which holds up youth as desirable, gears itself to making people feel old, and sets itself in prejudice against the elderly. If old is ugly, un-American, a sign of failure, and a "sin," there is much reason to fear its relentless "approach," its "attack," and its "victory."

The fact that aging is God-intended, and the only full-time work everyone does as long as he or she lives, is unconvincing when the mind and heart are set against it in fear and frustration. So it is possible to live at the edge of the frontier, positioned with one's back to it, or running away from it as long as possible. All the while the frontier remains, expands, and awaits our courage to create something with the God-given gifts and ingenuity we have as people who worship and serve a wise and loving Creator/Father.

Research in the field of aging is a late arrival in science. Concerns for aging were first raised in connection with the treatment of disease, and thus led to the specialty of geriatrics. According to Birren (1964), the first major compendium was published in 1939 *(Problems of Aging,* edited by E. V. Cowdry). Although originating with the United States Public Health Service, the creation of a unit on gerontology (a branch of knowledge dealing with aging and the problems of the aged) allowed for a wider-scoped focus which included sociological and psychological concerns as well as biological and medical ones. The National Gerontological Society was founded in 1945 to stimulate and correlate information in the whole field of aging.

It has already been noted that Maves and Cedarleaf made the first comprehensive study of the relationship of the Protestant churches to people over sixty years of age. Their work was conducted between 1946 and 1948 under the sponsorship of the Department of Pastoral Services of the Federal Council of Churches of Christ in America.

It is important for us to consider the realities of the frontier of aging, its size, nature, problems, and possibilities, if we are to move effectively into it. Therefore, it is necessary to scout out the land.

The place to begin is with a definition of aging. Contrary to the popular view of aging, which makes it a state of being, gerontologists declare it to be a life process.

DEFINITION OF AGING

A realistic definition might be: "Aging refers to the process of change in the organism from the time of fertilization of the ovum until death of the individual" (Lansing, 1959).

Others promote an illness model which limits their definition to the deterioration process which takes place in a mature organism over a period of time and ultimately leads to death.

Chronological factors were once primary in the consideration of aging and the definition of what is old. That concept has now been outgrown. The only current use of chronology is in terms of general reference to aging, and to demographic data. For cultural purposes, dates and years are given or required. Culturally, we may define a person as being "old" when the fifty-fifth, sixtieth, or sixty-fifth year is reached. The line is usually drawn at age sixty-five, the time of mandatory retirement for many.

Our youth-oriented culture takes chronology seriously. It beholds time as the great enemy, eroder of the possibilities for opportunities and meaning. In the time spectrum of our society, to reach age 30 is to be "over the hill." On the other hand, pre-retirement counseling and preparation is suggested as early as age 35. Middle age is entered between forty and fifty and continues from 50 to 60. Gerontologists declare the "young old" are those between 60 and 75; the "middle old" between 75 and 85; and the "old old" those 85 and beyond.

DEMOGRAPHIC DATA

Using the chronological measuring stick, the only one we have for demographic data, we find that the number of persons 65 and older is large and growing. It is this that makes the new frontier so vast.

Between 1900 and 1960, the population of the United States increased 250 percent. In the same period, the population of those aged sixty-five and over increased 500 percent. Put in numbers, nearly 23 million, or more than 10 percent, are sixty-five and older. The number is growing at a net rate of 900 per day. More than 70 percent of the 65 plus age group have reached retirement age in the last ten years. By 1980, twelve percent of the population will be 65 years of age and older.

One gerontologist acknowledges that while the increase in the number of persons over 65 will be only eight million between 1970 and 1990, by the year 2020, the number is expected to double. Other specialists in demography forecast over 50 percent of the population will be over age fifty by the year 2000. At that time the four- and five-generation family which is now appearing, will become more the norm.

In light of these statistics, it should be emphasized that only about 5 percent of the nearly 23 million aged in America are in full-term custodial care. Most older persons are living independently, with varying degrees of life-satisfaction and feelings of well-being, in spite of the many problems they face which tend to become enlarged or inflated with the passing of time.

FACTORS IN AGING

The question arises, if chronological aging is not the most important determinant or measure of aging, what other factors are considered to be more important? Gerontologists identify several kinds of aging, individually identifiable but usually interelated.

Biological Aging. Biological aging refers to changes in cellular composition and capacity for growth. Scientists working in this field focus on tissue structure and function, and in the strength, speed, and endurance of the neuro-muscular system. They measure the reduction in the ability to integrate organ systems, believing that maximum strength is reached between the ages of 25 to 30 years. Among frequently noted physical changes are: changes in vision and hearing; skin changes; loss of dentition; loss of hair; decreased immunity; impairment of memory for recent events; decreased muscle mass and tone; decreased energy and tolerance for exercise; and decreased sexual activity.

Psychological Aging. Psychological aging refers to changes in personality. Depending on the general mental health of the person and the ability to respond with resiliency in the face of multiple losses, psychological aging may or may not be a significant factor in a person's aging. There seem to be two possibilities for the aging person. Either he or she matures and grows, or deteriorates and is dehumanized, with the possibility always present for movement in either direction. Symptoms of aging increase and may cause premature aging if the deterioration of interests takes over.

Sociological Aging. Sociological aging has to do with changing circumstances of an individual in family, community, and society. Social age refers to the social habits and roles of the individual relative to the expectations of his group and society. Problems are raised for the older American because of the required relinquishment of certain roles at a relatively early age. A long span of years devoid of social meaning may take their toll in a sense of normlessness, giving rise to apathy and futility. Those who adapt well to their changing environment are socially alive, while those who are unable to adjust find themselves isolated and brittle.

Behavioral Aging. Behavioral aging is concerned with the issues of self-image, feeling, and the tolerance of stress. The subjective feeling of health, or well-being, is important to one's self-image. Personality-style, which is one's coping style and ability, is highly important to the rate and degree of aging. Each person is unique in behavioral aging because he or she is unique in personality and experience.

Chronic brain syndrome, popularly known as "senility," is a condition which arouses great concern in most persons. While senility has been customarily thought to be the result of physiological deterioration and/or accidents, there is growing evidence and conviction that emotional, relational, and cultural factors are more frequent culprits in inducing chronic brain syndrome. One gerontologist states:

> Senility is only the lack of challenge from the environment. Senility is the inward turning and the forgetting because it is all so awkward and so clumsy and so terribly unexciting to be on the shelf (Peterson, taped address).

MISCONCEPTIONS, STEREOTYPES AND MYTHS

Specialists in the field of aging report a series of misconceptions, myths, and stereotypes common in our culture. One such list (there are others, or one can make his or her own) is as follows:

> Most of the aged are ill or disabled.
>
> Most aged have no sexual interest or activity.
>
> Most aged suffer from serious mental deterioration and "senility."
>
> Employment and productivity of older workers is low.
>
> Older people will not change.
>
> Older people are like children.
>
> Older people belong in one group.
>
> Physical limitations imply inability to function (Leanse and Jacobs, 1972 pp. 3-5).

Ethel Percy Andrus, Founder and President of the National Retired Teachers Association and the American Association of Retired Persons, addressed this condition when she asked, "How to change the stereotype of aging to that of dynamic maturity? How to bring beauty to being old? How to begin the authenticity of age? These are our challenges" (Crippen, *et al.,* eds, 1968 p. 185).

TOWARD A REALISTIC VIEW OF AGING

As if to make a beginning response to the question raised by Dr. Andrus, Jean Maxwell, in her handbook, *Centers for Older People* (1962), offered this perspective:

> From the gerontological knowledge and research the following ideas have emerged:
>
> Aging is universal.
>
> Aging is normal.
>
> Aging is variable.
>
> Dying is normal and inevitable.
>
> Aging and illness are not necessarily coincidental.
>
> Older people represent three generations (65-75, 75-85, and 85 and beyond).
>
> Older people can and do learn.
>
> Older people want to remain self-directing.
>
> Older people are vital human beings (pp. 12-13).

CONTINUITY AND CHANGE

It is a matter of fact that every person is in a continuing "process of becoming" as the adventure of living is made through the multiple transitions of life.

In light of modern research, Tolstoy was close to the mark:

> I remember very vividly that I am conscious of myself in exactly the same way now, at 81, as I was conscious of myself, my "I," at five or six years of age. Consciousness is immovable. Due to this alone there is a movement which we call "time." If time moves on, then there must be something that stands still, the consciousness of my "I" stands still (Butler 1974, pp. 104-105).

We are being taught to recognize and to expect that the older a person becomes, the more unique is his or her personality. Aging is not a leveler of individual differences.

Rather, it is the means by which one becomes increasingly like oneself in attitude, interest, and action.

PROBLEMS OF AGING

The older person in the United States typically faces problems that are more numerous, more serious, and more strange to him than any he has faced since his adolescence and early adulthood.

Two researchers (Clark and Anderson, 1967, p. 60) reported results from a study conducted in 1959 in San Francisco concerning the main problems of older people. Seven themes emerged:

1. A change in physical appearance.
2. Partial or total retirement from active duties.
3. Lower energy level.
4. Greater possibility of ill health.
5. Greater possibility of need of help.
6. Changes in cognitive and intellectual functioning.
7. Greater uncertainty about the duration of life.

These were considered to be areas of potential stress and threats to one's equilibrium.

In his book, *Why Survive: Being Old in America,* Robert N. Butler (1975) updates and outlines the comprehensive personal and social problems older people meet.

Most gerontologists define the problems of the aging and the aged in terms of *loss.* As each person moves through life, losses small and great occur, and have their effects upon the individual. Compensations must be made if the person is to live with dignity, meaning, and satisfaction. One specialist enumerates possible *common losses: loss* of physical faculties (i.e., acuity of vision and hearing); *loss* of one's instrumental role in society (perhaps through compulsory retirement); *loss* of prestige due to loss of mastery; *loss* of authority with one's children; *loss* of close ties with loved ones due to death; *loss* of home and freedom; *loss* of an everlasting future on this earth, in which one can undo what one has done and in which one can still do what one has failed to do so far (Ujhely, 1968, pp. 25-26).

In addition, there is a subtle aspect to the problems of aging; the lack of preparedness on the part of many for the long years they are called to live following retirement.

Isolation is a devastating problem for many older persons. It may be thrust upon a person by rejection or lack of appreciation by family, friends, or society. It may be the result of withdrawal chosen by a hurt and weakened spirit unable to cope with the overwhelming demands of an unkind society. It is believed that some people isolate themselves to preserve the illusion of independence.

Cultural Deprivation. The problem of cultural deprivation has been noted as an inescapable reality which rears its head for all who have eyes to see. Commitment to staying young, coupled with fear of aging, has resulted in deprivation of older people on many levels of American life. Stereotypes give birth to prejudice. Prejudice spawns negativism. Negativism issues in outright attitudes and action which "put down" older persons. "Old is bad" is bred into our citizens and reinforced by cultural values and directions. A no deposit-no return spirit extends beyond things to people, and has its most denigrating effect upon older persons.

Many trace this condition to the Protestant Work Ethic, which demands that one must "produce" to be acceptable. Since many older persons are unable to produce in work that adds to monetary value, and since leisure and rest are secondary values in our society, discriminatory devices arise to plague older persons.

Discrimination appears in many guises. Not only are many aging persons fearful of the aging process, but they learn to expect and accept discrimination against them. They are their own worst enemies, having bought what the culture has been selling about older people — worthlessness and rejection.

Specific discrimination is traceable in medical care, ignorance, and neglect. The problem of "putting down" the older person has long-range societal effects. Not only does the older person suffer, but young people enter the process of rejecting their own aging, with the net result of unwillingness of persons to plan for their old age.

Alex Comfort (1976) defines cultural deprivation of

older persons as "agism," and calls for overcoming its ravaging effects:

> Agism is the notion that people cease to be people, cease to be the same people or become people of a distinct and inferior kind, by virtue of having lived a specific number of years. The eighteenth century French naturalist Georges Buffon said, "to the philosopher, old age must be considered a prejudice." Agism is that prejudice. Like racism, which it resembles, it is based on fear, folklore, and the hangups of a few unlovable people who propagate these. Like racism, it needs to be met by information, contradiction and when necessary, confrontation. And the people who are being victimized have to stand up for themselves in order to put it down (p. 35).

NEEDS OF AGING

The needs of the aging are really the needs of persons of every age, only magnified. One sociologist reports a historical perspective of five wishes of old folk everywhere: to live as long as possible; to hoard waning energies; to keep on sharing in the affairs of life; to safeguard any seniority rights; and to have an honorable release from life if possible.

Clark Tibbitts, one of the earliest leaders in gerontological research, reported five needs which should be satisfied if persons are to grow old gracefully: the need for relatedness or association with others; the need for creativity; the need for security; the need for individuality or recognition; and the need for orientation or an intellectual frame of reference. In this case we might agree that the needs of the aging are the needs of every person, only heightened.

The author perceives that persons have both what may be called "bread needs" and "beyond bread needs" which must be met if life-satisfaction is to come while growing older.

Bread Needs. Sociologists have been concerned for several basic "survival" needs of older persons. Money, health (including nutrition and health care), housing, transportation, and services are recognized as being of primary importance. The 1971 White House Conference on Aging dealt with these as well as with legal, retirement, and employment needs, all of which might be considered "bread needs." Many government programs are aimed at meeting these needs on national, state, and local levels.

While the church/ synagogue must have concern for the meeting of "bread needs," there are other needs for which they must have special concern; these may be called "beyond bread needs."

Beyond Bread Needs. The primary focus of this book is on the "beyond bread needs" of older persons and how these needs might be met for the renewal and fulfillment of older persons.

The Judeo-Christian faith boldly states, ". . . man shall not live by bread alone . . .." First recorded in the book of Deuteronomy (Chapter 8, verse 3b), it was recycled by Jesus of Nazareth as recorded in Matthew 4:4; and in Luke 4:4. All the bread in the world cannot meet the beyond bread needs of persons of any age!

The issue arising in consideration of the needs of older persons is that more than the meeting of physical needs is essential to the happiness and well-being of persons. What are the "beyond bread needs" of older persons and what is, can, and should be, done about meeting them?

Clues have come largely through contemporary secular rather than religious sources. Erich Fromm, Erik Erikson, Abraham Maslow, Marjorie Fiske Lowenthal, to name a few, have addressed themselves to aspects of other than physical needs of human beings. From the religious community, Howard Clinebell, Jr. and Charlotte H. Clineball have added an important concern.

Fromm (1955) dealt with five basic non-physical needs which persist throughout the life-cycle: a sense of identity; the need for relatedness or belonging; the need for rootedness (some place, geographical location, or spiritual concept to which one can feel attached); the need for transcendence of time-limited existence; and the need for a frame of reference to organize life which helps give it meaning.

Erikson (1963) outlined "eight stages of man" as being normative in the life-process from birth to old age. "Ego integrity" is the name he gave to the eighth, or final stage in which the person puts together all of the pieces of his or her life and finds meaning inherent in his/her own existence. Lack or loss of ego-integrity is signified by death for the person who has been unable to accept his or her life-cycle as an ultimate in life. Despair is the unblessing of the person who fails to achieve or retain integrity. The eight stages for Erikson are evolutionary, interrelated, and inter-dependent, each necessary for the next.

Maslow (1954) gave us the concept and term "self-actualization." He presents what he terms a "hierarchy of needs" in each person. Physiological or survival needs (food, housing, clothing, health care, mobility); safety needs (security, protection against physical threats, familiarity, and stability of the environment); belonging needs (affection, inclusion in one's group); esteem needs (adequacy, competence, achievement, contribution, recognition, prestige); and finally self-actualization needs (becoming one's self by developing to one's fullest capacity as a human being; finding meaning in life and answers to life's questions). Maslow declared these needs to be in an ascending order as stated. He believed that for the most part, they are not fully met in a given person; also they are both conscious and unconscious.

Lowenthal (1968) has worked in the area of relational support over many years with isolated and lonely persons. Findings from her studies indicate the need of a "confidant" with whom a person, particularly an older person, can share his or her deepest experiences and needs. Such a resource serves as a buffer against the losses which come through reduction of role and social interaction. The person who has no confidant, family member or friend, tends to function less well, and often is subject to depression and other emotional problems.

Howard J. Clinebell, Jr., and Charlotte H. Clinebell (1970) developed a concept of the importance of relating. Patterning the title after Sigmund Freud's "will to pleasure" or Alfred Adler's "will to power" or Viktor Frankl's "will to meaning," they chose "the will to relate." Based on studies of personality, the "will to relate" is declared to be the most basic human striving, upon the fulfillment of which other satisfactions depend.

SPIRITUAL WELL-BEING

The most obvious "beyond bread need" is spiritual well-being. Paul B. Maves and David O. Moberg have done more consistent work in the area of spiritual needs of older persons than perhaps any others. Maves includes in his book (1953) a witness by a physician, as regards the church. "In its affirmation of emotional and spiritual values as the food of life, it has always preached what psychoanalysis has rediscovered: that man does not live by bread alone, but by the symbolic meaning of what is given materially" (pp. 16-17).

Moberg is the apostle of spiritual well-being, having studied the subject from many perspectives, and having served as chairman of the committee that prepared the background material on that subject for the 1971 White House Conference on Aging.

He identified six areas of spiritual need as deserving special attention:

1. Sociocultural Sources of Spiritual Needs
2. Relief from Anxieties and Fears
3. Preparation for Death
4. Personality Integration
5. Personal Dignity
6. A Philosophy of Life (pp. 6-14).

Moberg also declares, "Man is a spiritual being and therefore can not live by bread alone" (1973).

Both Maves and Moberg view spiritual needs and spiritual well-being as relating to the totality of human need, taking seriously both "bread needs" and "beyond bread needs."

The National Interfaith Coalition on Aging, which grew out of the 1971 White House Conference on Aging, adopted its own definition of spiritual well-being on April 29, 1975. Representatives of Roman Catholic, Eastern Orthodox, Jewish, and Protestant religious bodies related to NICA, presented this definition to its constituents for study and guidance: "Spiritual well-being is the affirmation of life in a relationship with God, self, community, and environment that nurtures and celebrates wholeness."

The definition was declared and tested in the first National Intra-Decade Conference on Spiritual Well-Being and the Elderly, April 12-14, 1977, in Atlanta, Georgia. The author was in attendance and presented selected material from this book.

BIBLICAL AND THEOLOGICAL CONTRIBUTIONS

Biblical material predates all other contributions to the literature on aging. The Scriptures of the Old and New Testaments are not necessarily consistent in their approach to aging, nor do they pursue the subject of age or aging in an extended way. In the Old Testament, especially, different perspectives are offered. However, the prevailing thought is favorable to age. The basic belief is that aging produces understanding and wisdom, two of the most treasured accomplishments to be won by human effort, with divine assistance. Age is to be more esteemed than feared or disparaged. An examination of a Biblical concordance provides useful background and some interesting surprises.

Four passages are of unusual value:

> Do not cast me off in the time of old age; forsake me not when my strength is spent. Psalm 71:9. (RSV)

> Even youths shall faint and be weary, and young men shall fall exhausted; but they who wait for the Lord shall renew their strength, they shall mount up with wings like eagles, they shall run and not be weary, they shall walk and not faint. Isaiah 40:30-31. (RSV)

> Though our outer nature is wasting away, our inner nature is being renewed every day. II Corinthians 4:16. (RSV)

> In my Father's house are many rooms; if it were not so, would I have told you that I go to prepare a place for you? And when I go and prepare a place for you, I will come again and take you to myself, that where I am you may be also. John 14:2-3. (RSV)

THEOLOGICAL CONTRIBUTIONS

Perhaps the most surprising discovery made by the author in his study is the lack of a comprehensive theology of aging. Several persons have alluded to a theology that relates to aging and the aged in brief papers. A helpful report by the Texas Conference of Churches was developed as a position paper (1974). A special issue of the reconstituted *Pastoral Psychology* focused on the subject, "Toward a Theology of Aging," with Seward Hiltner serving as guest editor (1975).

From the Christian perspective, Carl G. Howie's paper, "Theology for Aging" (1977), presented at the National Intra-Decade Conference on Spiritual Well-Being and the Elderly, represents careful thought. None, however, is comprehensive. All are mere beginnings in an area truly the prerogative of the religious sector. James A. Peterson (n.d.), long involved in concern for the elderly, has stated:

> There is no theology of aging. One assumes that God is old, that his wisdom represents the accretion of the ages, and that he cherishes those who have done his work on earth for the kingdom of love. One finds nothing in the Scriptures to indicate that either grace or revelation is age-graded. But the Church has not developed either an exegetical or theological interest in undergirding older persons with a conceptual framework (p. 4).

An obvious beginning place for a sound theology of aging lies in the recognition, exposure and treatment of "agism" as a biblical and theological heresy. Coupled with the perception of Rabbi Robert L. Katz (1975), we have an open door for profound engagement with the issue from the Judeo-Christian point of view:

> Life becomes an unending Sabbath for the individual attaining the years of maturity; it persists for him until the day of his death. Nothing captures the essence of the theology of aging in Judaism as does the concept of aging as the Sabbath of the soul with its rich possibilities for self-realization (p. 148).

It seems incredible that the oldest institution and community dealing with human life should not have made this study again and again, revising material as new insights came. No doubt one of the reasons is that this is a new frontier, and that the church/synagogue as part of the culture has not been more creative than other parts. In this area, it seems to have followed rather than lead in the last forty years.

On the other hand, some denominations over a period of years, have made studies related to aging which might be available on request. It is the feeling of the author that these materials have largely been stored and filed, their contents unknown to the judicatories of the church and to local congregations, because no plan for disseminating them or training leaders with them has been made or implemented.

ROLE OF THE CHURCHES/SYNAGOGUES

There are signs that consciousness-raising is being done among the people of faith. Those who write from this perspective agree that churches/synagogues are institutions which usually combine service to the total person with concern for the whole society. They see the churches/ synagogues as the places where older people are most likely to be emotionally involved and, therefore, as having a special responsibility to consider the total person throughout the aging process.

But there must be a beginning place. One very convincing way of experiencing the aging frontier existentially is in the mirror — especially in daylight! As religious leaders, we need to come to terms with our own aging, and perhaps with our own gerontophobia. Then we may be able to address it positively, drawing upon the spiritual resources God has given and will give us to make our contribution among the people we serve.

Two strong statements are chosen from among many which may help us move ahead. Alone and together, they lay before us the challenge we must hear and act upon as the people of God:

> A human being would certainly not grow to be seventy or eighty years old if this longevity had no meaning for the species. The afternoon of human life must also have a significance of its own and cannot be merely a pitiful appendage to life's morning (June, 1971, p. 17).

> If our religious institutions do not actively and specifically take on the spiritual needs of mankind as a primary responsibility, it may be that no other institution in society will. After all, there is only one thing that churches and other religious bodies can do best. That one thing is to accentuate the spiritual well-being of the elderly lest it be overlooked completely. Man is a spiritual being and therefore can not live by bread alone. If the churches and synagogues of our land offer only bread, even the bread they offer is likely to turn to stone (Moberg, 1973, pp. 3).

REFERENCES

Birren, James E. (ed.) "Principles of Research on Aging," in *Handbook of Aging and the Individual: Psychological and Biological Aspects.* Chicago: The University of Chicago Press, 1964.

Booth, Gotthard. "Health from the Standpoint of the Physician," in Maves, Paul B., *The Church and Mental Health.* New York: Charles Scribner's Sons, 1953.

Butler, Robert N. "The Creative Life and Old Age," in Pfeiffer, Eric, M.D., *Successful Aging.* Center for the Study of Aging and Human Development, Duke University, Durham, North Carolina, 1974.

Butler, Robert N. *Why Survive? Being Old in America.* New York: Harper and Row, 1975.

Clark, Margaret and Anderson, Barbara G. *Culture and Aging.* Springfield, Illinois: Charles C. Thomas, 1967.

Clinebell, Howard J. And Clinebell, Charlotte H. *The Intimate Marriage.* New York: Harper and Row, 1970.

Comfort, Alex. *A Good Age.* New York: Crown Publishers, Inc., 1976.

Crippen, Dorothy, *et al.* (eds) *The Wisdom of Ethel Percy Andrus.* Long Beach, California: NRTA/AARP 1968.

Erikson, Erik. *Childhood and Society.* New York: W. W. Norton and Co., 1963.

Fromm, Erich. *The Sane Society.* New York: Rinehart, 1955.

Hiltner, Seward. (ed.) *Toward a Theology of Aging.* New York: Human Science Press, 1975.

Howie, Carl G. *Theology for Aging.* Paper presented at the National Intra-Decade Conference on Spiritual Well-Being and the Elderly, Atlanta, Georgia, 1977.

Jung, Carl G. "The Stages of Life," in Campbell, Joseph (ed.) *The Portable Jung.* New York: Viking Press, 1971.

Katz, Robert L. "Jewish Values and Sociopsychological Perspectives on Aging," *Pastoral Psychology,* XXIV (Winter, 1975), Number 229,

Lansing, Albert "General Biology of Senescence," in Birren, James E. (ed.) *Handbook of Aging and the Individual.* Chicago: University of Chicago Press, 1964.

Leanse, Joyce and Jacobs, Bella. *Working with Older People.* The National Council on the Aging, Inc., Washington, D.C., 1972.

Lowenthal, Marjorie F. and Haven, Clayton. "Interaction and Adaptation: Intimacy as a Critical Variable," in Neugarten, Beatrice L., *Middle Age and Aging.* Chicago: University of Chicago Press, 1968.

Maslow, Abraham H. *Motivation and Personality.* New York: Harper and Row, 1954.

Maxwell, Jean M. *Centers for Older People.* The National Council on the Aging, Washington, D.C., 1962.

Moberg, David O. *Spiritual Well-Being.* White House Conference on Aging, Washington, D.C., 1971.

――――――――――――― . "The Church/Synagogue Hearing the Challenge," in *Making the Knowledge Explosion Work for the Elderly.* 19th Annual Meeting, Western Gerontological Society, April 29-May 1, 1973.

Peterson, James A. "Overview in the Field of Aging," an addressed taped at the meeting of the Southern California Interfaith Coalition on Aging Conference, Los Angeles, California, December 2, 1975.

Peterson, James A., quoted by Earl M. Kragnes, Coordinator, Church Relations, NRTA, AARP, Washington, D.C. Mimeographed speech untitled, n.d.

The Church and the Aging. A Position Paper by the Texas Conference of Churches, Austin, Texas, June 1974.

Tibbitts, Clark. "Creating a Climate for the Middle Years," in Tibbitts, C. and Donahue, W. (eds.) *Aging in Today's Society,* Englewood Cliffs, N.J.: Prentice Hall, 1960.

Ujhely, Gertrude B. "Nursing Assessment of Psycho-Social Function in the Aged," in *Nursing Assessment of the Aged.* Third Annual Daniel Rubenstein Lectureship in Gerontology, Boston College, October 28, 1968.

3 Occupying The Territory

Having scouted out the land of the new frontier, in which the size, nature, problems, and possibilities of ministry and the aging have been considered, the next step is to discover how the territory is being occupied.

WHAT IS BEING DONE?

Much debate has occurred over the years as to whether older persons should be separated into groups which reflect their age. Often voices are raised that it is wrong to put them into such categories, with the plea for more inter-generational exposure and activity. While opportunity for such experiences probably happens most naturally and regularly in the religious community, at least in some parts of its life (i.e., worship, congregational dinners, picnics, etc.), given the realities of the culture, it appears that most persons of any age find friends and support in groups of persons of similar age.

Some sociologists have found that most older people have more friends who are older than younger. This observation supports a growing concern that older persons tend to find peer relationships that produce renewal possibilities which can lead to fulfillment. The church/synagogue has an important responsibility in this concern and should attempt to help it happen. On the other hand, care must be taken not to put older people still further out of communication with other groups. They need to be in touch with the real interests and issues of the world of which they can still be a part.

Secular Centers. Perhaps the most significant work among older people, on a large scale, has been done, and is now being done, through the multi-purpose Senior Centers related to the National Institute of Senior Centers. The first known center for older people came into being in 1944 in New York City. The term "Center" may mean whatever any person or group wishes it to mean. However, a general consensus as outlined in *Centers for Older People* (Maxwell, 1962), is that a "Center" is a designated place in which older people meet at least two days or more each week, under the guidance of paid leaders performing professional tasks. The multi-purpose center focuses on basic needs such as food, shelter, clothing, health care, transportation, recreation, companionship and love, and a purpose to living. The *1974 Directory of Senior Centers and Clubs: A National Resource,* listed approximately 4,900 programs and important other data.

Church Programs and Centers. The community-accepted definition of "Center" as just described need not dissuade the religious community. There is no reason to limit the use of the word "Center" in regard to churches and synagogues. A "Center" may be any place where persons gather to give and receive the good things of life. One promising option for us, then, is to create "Centers" using our own local resources. Professional leadership is desireable but not essential. What is essential is a well-conceived and well-conducted program which is broad enough to meet many of the needs of persons, and their own involvement in the planning and conducting of the "Center's" life.

The value of a "Center" lies in its benefits for older persons which are in addition to intergenerational experiences in family, church, or community groups. Advantages usually include: (1) a planned spectrum of programs to meet broad-scoped interests; (2) continued input on a regular basis; and (3) physical, mental, and emotional stimulation through exposure, sharing, and learning.

On the other hand, we must recognize open prejudice to "Centers" due to: (1) ignorance of their purpose and program; (2) stereotyped convictions that such places are for ghettoizing the feeble in mind and body; (3) general resistance to identification with aging and the aged; and (4) reluctance of many older persons to becoming involved and stimulated.

While many congregations do "something" concerning older persons, most programs seem to deal with bits and pieces. Few seem to have caught the holistic sense of need and opportunity and to develop programs which represent and reflect that vision and concern. Some of the reasons for this condition have already been stated. A brief comparison between secular "Centers" and congregational "Centers" and programs may help to increase understanding and stimulate action in the religious sector.

Due to several factors, the secular sector has moved ahead more rapidly and effectively than the religious sector. Among these factors are: (1) the recognition by specialists in gerontology of the needs of older people as revealed through research; (2) funds made available through taxation and administered by governmental agencies; (3) leadership development and support provided by public money; and (4) program development and evaluation made possible by funds committed for this special purpose and carried on by trained professionals whose careers are dedicated to this field.

On the other hand, the church and synagogue have proceeded on another course which includes such factors as: (1) lack of awareness of the needs of older persons; (2) failure to consider older persons as a priority concern; (3) limited funds to cover a wide-scoped ministry for all ages, and to the mission beyond the local congregation and community; (4) lack of trained leadership, both professional and volunteer in the field of aging; (5) lack of a comprehensive theology of aging; (6) lack of denominationally-sponsored materials and training opportunities; and (7) busy schedules of pastors, priests, and rabbis who must be "generalists," and are uncomfortable in the field of aging and the aged.

The general feeling has thus emerged in the culture (except perhaps for those working in gerontology or other sociological and psychological fields), and is often reflected in the churches and synagogues that:

Older people have "had it."

Older people don't "need it."

Older people aren't "worth it."

Nothing significant can be done.

The end result is a vicious circle which needs to be broken. The question is who shall break it, and how shall it be done?

WHAT NEEDS TO BE DONE?

Basic to moving ahead is the courage to confess that too little has been done, and is now being done by most congregations, small and large, in ministry among older persons. Professional leaders of congregations (pastors, priests, rabbis) must be courageous enough to search their consciences (this may be done together in workshops and training conferences where the possibility of improvement and learning for action can replace guilt, frustration, and inadequacy). Leaders in the religious sector must face the fact that most of what is being done is in bits and pieces and is probably uninformed, either by Biblical and theological reflection on this need, or by insights coming from gerontological research and practice. Apathy and reluctance to enter the field by faith, and in good will must be overcome by a new awareness of calling to this ministry in an aging nation, and in aging congregations.

Few congregations have been ready to evaluate their programs among older persons, testing their effectiveness so that better ones can emerge. The "scientific approach" has been left to the secularists, while the "spiritual approach" has been the fortress of the people of faith. The two have seldom met, and when they have it usually has been with prejudice, tentativeness and, sometimes, disdain. Each needs the other.

That will come as each is willing to enter the other's world for learning and involvement to improve society by bettering the image and conditions of the aging and the aged. Both sides stand to lose if we fail in this endeavor.

This book is an attempt at a breakthrough toward meeting the need. The overview of aging offered and the specific helps outlined are toward this end. The appeal is made to the sensitivity of religious colleagues at the grass roots level to the needs and possibilities of older persons. The emphasis is on the total picture, allowing and encouraging the reader to begin where he or she is and to move forward in ways which will not prove to be detours or dead-end streets, but will lead to progress and growth for all.

BASIC FACTORS TO CONSIDER

Here are the basic factors in approaching possibilities for effective ministry among older persons: (1) the global needs of older persons; (2) a constellation of factors basic to understanding and working with older persons; (3) the importance of renewal and fulfillment; (4) definition of renewal and fulfillment; (5) ways of achieving renewal and fulfillment; and (6) signs of renewal and fulfillment.

Global Needs of Older Persons. Attention has already been given to both the "bread needs" and "beyond bread needs" of older persons. Taken together, they may be considered to be "global needs" which every person experiences. Sometimes the needs are latent or "quiet;" sometimes they are immediate and urgent. Spiritual well-being may be taken to mean a feeling of satisfaction that these needs are being met, or are at least in the process of being met. James E. Birren (1964) considers the individual as ". . . a biological, psychological, and social constellation, moving forward in time" (p. 1). Those who wish to work effectively among older persons must be aware of the global needs of older persons, endeavor to understand the persons and these needs, and desire to assist the persons in understanding and meeting their needs.

CONSTELLATION OF FACTORS BASIC TO UNDERSTANDING AND WORKING WITH OLDER PERSONS

In addition to the global needs of individuals, a constellation of factors basic to understanding and working with older persons must be considered. The factors are brought to light through gerontological research and investigation. While usually treated separately in literature and practice, they are presented here in a cluster so that the reader may sense their individual importance and inter-relationship. If renewal and fulfillment are to take place in older persons, both the global needs and the following constellation of factors must be kept before our attention as realities with which we must deal:

1. Social factors impacting the person must be acknowledged: i.e., ethnic, financial, social status, geographic location, family relationships.

2. Pre-retirement patterns of life-style including the degree of fulfillment achieved before retirement.

3. Physical and mental health, which may depend upon the degree of self-esteem of the person, are profound elements.

4. Personality-type, or coping style, is perhaps the most significant determinant, as it tends to increasing uniqueness over the life span.

5. Opportunity for self-development and expression through intake and output is a strong ingredient.

6. The degree of disengagement or involvement has a significant place, and may depend on personality-style or health factors.

7. Religious faith and practice, if any, must interrelate with all of these.

There is much untravelled territory in every human being. It is obvious that we are working with realities which are probably more complex than we have realized, even though we may have inwardly sensed the profundity of it all. It is clear that there is no easy answer to such an intertwined skein of needs and factors. The call is to a quest, to make a beginning toward doing something necessary and useful, or having begun, to continue with greater commitment and effectiveness, gathering light and strength as we go.

The Importance of Renewal and Fulfillment. All roads lead to renewal and fulfillment as a central need for older persons. That is, how shall they compensate for increasing losses, and often mounting needs so that their lives can be satisfying to the end? Studies show that earlier fulfillment in life holds promise for later fulfillment, and vice versa. They also indicate that fulfillment is a personal matter, varying with each individual. Some persons need more "pay-offs" than others to give them a sense of movement toward fulfillment. It has been shown, as well as being a matter of common sense, that older persons must take responsibility for themselves in order to experience renewal and fulfillment. Talents must be used and gifts exercised in order to feel healthy and to experience self-worth. "Capacities clamor to be used and cease their clamor only when they are used sufficiently . . . capacities are needs, and therefore are intrinsic values as well . . ." (Maslow, 1968, p. 152). But the question arises, how can this be accomplished? And what is renewal? What is fulfillment?

DEFINITIONS OF "RENEWAL" AND "FULFILLMENT"

"Renewal" is the maintenance, recovery, or discovery of incentive to continue creatively in life. It is to have the desire to live meaningfully.

"Fulfillment" is the capability of dealing creatively with the tension between problems and potentials in such a way as to produce the positive feeling that one's life has continued meaning, direction, and promise of completion (Hiltner, 1960).

Renewal relates to fulfillment by keeping the incentive high enough to support the continuation of bearing the tension until the problems are met or are under way toward being met. Renewal supplies the emotional and social strength for working toward and through to fulfillment. Renewal is not an end in itself. Renewal is in order to fulfillment.

Some persons seem to be renewed without being fulfilled. It is impossible, on the other hand, for anyone to be fulfilled without being renewed. Therefore, renewal precedes fulfillment. Continuing fulfillment (spiritual well-being) gives meaning and purpose to life.

FACTORS IN RENEWAL AND FULFILLMENT

Renewal and fulfillment are dependent upon several factors, especially in the support of incentive to continued creativity in life. So renewal of incentive, or the desire to live meaningfully, can be achieved in three ways:

Maintenance. Maintenance of incentive seems to be all that is needed for some, perhaps for many. By continuing useful means, they are able to keep the level of motivation high enough to function well. No extraordinary emphasis seems to be necessary. But as food nourishes the body and must be regularly taken, so intake is necessary for mainte- nance of incentive. Transference of energy and substitution of satisfactions are "naturally" and easily handled by many people. But it must be understood that maintenance *is* renewal. Continuing relationships are one example of regular maintenance. We need to emphasize the importance of maintenance as the preferable way of upholding incentive to remain creatively interested in life.

Recovery. Recovery of incentive is a deep need for many who have lost or forfeited their ability and desire to live creatively. By withdrawing from the use of once-viable sources of maintaining motivation, because of loss, hurt, failure, or other cause, they feel "down" and "out," often useless, unwanted, ineffective, depressed, incapable of handl- ing life, unhappy with their lot. Recovery of incentive is the issue of basic concern for them, whether or not they recognize it as such or feel that recovery is possible.

The recovery process usually involves other people, and *always* demands the will to recover of the person who needs it. The process may be short or long, simple or involved, depending on the person and the circumstances. It may be quiet or dramatic, almost imperceptible or openly evident. But recovery, to be effective and lasting, must be sustained through maintenance.

Discovery. Discovery of incentive is a wonderful possibility for the person who has never felt the juices of renewal flowing in his or her life. It often comes as a serendipitous experience, arising from an unexpected activity or relationship, bringing with it the surprise which lifts the person to a new level of awareness of life and new possibilities for living with meaning.

Discovery may occur independently from maintenance or recovery, or it may be a sought-after ingredient to accompany, enrich, and sustain them. Discovery can become the way of life for the person who is aware of its power to get life moving again, or to keep it moving in exciting new directions.

A FURTHER WORD ABOUT FULFILLMENT

Fulfillment is getting on with handling life. It is more than being "equipped" to do this; it is onward, forward movement. When problems are met with adequate potential for resolution, working through, or even survival intent, a sense of fulfillment results. When potential is actually or preceptually inadequate, fulfillment fades. A sense of "impossibility" results. The person tends to move into a "no man's land" of frustration, loss, inadequacy, and perhaps anxiety, depression, or despair. The tension between problems and potential goes. Relief from pain over unresolved matters is sought through repression, withdrawal, alcohol, drugs, fantasy, or other means of escape.

SOURCES OF RENEWAL AND FULFILLMENT

In western culture, younger people seem to seek fulfillment in growth or expansion of one's powers. In mid-life, however, this understanding is threatened due to the inevitable decline of powers and potential. At this point, fulfillment begins to be understood through metaphors of depth rather than breadth, or a combination of both (Hiltner, 1960). Reuel L. Howe (1974) reinforces Hiltner's conclusion that fulfillment comes out of struggle.

There is no single solution for causing renewal and fulfillment. Every approach seems to require consistent effort, often of many kinds. Sometimes the work is done in terms of the old and familiar, and sometimes with the new and strange.

Several sources of renewal and filfillment seem to be useful.

Religious Faith. The importance of religious faith is perhaps the primary source of renewal and fulfillment for many older persons (and younger ones as well!). Its positive contributions cannot be overstated provided, of course, that the nature of the religious faith and practice produces wholeness, evidenced by emotional health and strength.

Faith, prayer, worship, reading the Bible and other religious literature, the sacraments, keeping of religious observances and ceremonies, honoring holy days and holidays, sacred music, sharing of life and faith experiences, giving service and money to God's Kingdom on earth, are all part of religious experience. There is therapy in talking, touching, in fasting and feasting. Regular engagement in religious faith and practice puts persons in touch with the God of creation and redemption, the Lord of Life, our Eternal Home.

Experience of Religious Community. Findings from a number of surveys indicate that fulfillment is achieved by individuals in and through community, rather than in isolation from one another. The community of faith holds the greatest potential for experiences of renewal and fulfillment because it expresses the relationship between God and persons, between persons and other persons, and between persons and themselves. People have been created to live and achieve creativity within their capacities. Taking into account their limitations, they may achieve this creativity through community, especially the community of faith. Therein the long story of believers in the Judeo-Christian tradition can be heard and shared, and lived out in present day circumstances.

Social Participation. Many studies of the life-satisfaction of older persons show that most people who are active in social involvement are happier than those who are not. Ethel Percy Andrus, founder of the NRTA/AARP, was a strong advocate of involvement through service. A sample of her philosophy, confirmed by her own life, reads:

> The goal today is to help older folk about us find again "a role in life," an active role that will restore those who are tending to withdraw into their memories and a self-enforced solitary retirement. The need is to challenge such people to participate mentally and physically in the mainstream of the life about them. (Crippen, *et al.*, 1968, p. 152)

Second Careers. Among the positive possibilities for many older persons is a "second career." Paul Tournier, M.D., Swiss psychiatrist and author, makes this a central focus of his book, *Learn to Grow Old* (1971), written out of his own experience of aging. A "second career" may be a continuation of one's first career, on a lesser demand basis. It may be something related to what one has done over the years of employment, or it may be something entirely new and different. The point of the "second career" is that is provides an opportunity for remaining in life, giving and receiving, using one's talents, or developing new ones, without the pressure of having to "make a living" or to keep a strict schedule. For many active people, the "second career" may well be a good path to renewal and fulfillment, especially if mandatory retirement is experienced as a significant loss.

Ministry of Older Persons. The ministry of older persons looms as a bright possibility both for them and for their congregations. Every community of believers is in need of the wealth of experience, wisdom, skills, talents, time, and energy stored up in its older members. The experience of renewal and fulfillment awaiting many older persons through their own ministries cannot be estimated! Not only will they and their congregations profit by such endeavor, society needs their services. What brighter hope can young people behold than to see older persons happily and usefully engaged in causes which benefit our whole country's life? Good literature is available in the form of handbooks to assist leaders in discovering and using the resources of older persons (see Bibliography for suggestions).

SIGNS OF RENEWAL AND FULFILLMENT

Renewal and fulfillment are more than dreams or concepts. They are demonstrated realities for some who are willing and able to employ the resources described in this book. In spite of the fact that we live in a no deposit-no return culture, some of the definable and recognizable signs of renewal and fulfillment in older persons are:

Motivation — the ability to continue in life without boredom, apathy, or withdrawal.

Physical improvement — where possible, movement away from worry and disability, to acceptance of limitation and/or regained vigor.

Creativity — continuation or renaissance of interest and activity leading to positive use of time, energy, and skills, rather than the seeking of amusement, diversion, or commitment to killing time.

Competence — adequacy and enjoyment in doing what a person wishes to do.

Confidence — the feeling of well-being, based on the assurance of one's ability to have an effect on one's world.

Satisfaction — inner happiness based on the belief, "I am still enjoying life, knowing I am a unique person, able to function within my limitations and options."

Purpose — sense of meaning and direction in life that leads to a belief in full completion.

Expectation — ability to live in the present while looking ahead with confidence that the best, even beyond this life, is yet to be.

As if to help us in the family of faith understand what is needed in ministry and older people, the Kansas State Department of Social Welfare, Division of Social Services for the Aging, prepared a document (1968) which issues a clear call:

The Church has an innate obligation to take an interest in the older persons within its congregations and in the community . . . Services of a spiritual nature are not enough; there must be a combination of services which meet the spiritual, social, and physical needs. Words without actions can be very disenchanting to the older

person and very misleading to the younger person . . .
Above all, planning programs must hinge upon listening to
the real concerns and feelings of the aging themselves . . .
They need to participate in creative investments rather than
be handed a "canned" program. (p. 29)

Attention is now turned to a specific situation in which
the appeal just stated for the renewal and fulfillment of older
persons was sought through an action/investigation project.

REFERENCES

Birren, James E. *The Psychology of Aging.* Englewood Cliffs, New
    Jersey: Prentice-Hall, Inc., 1964.
Crippen, Dorothy, *et al.,* (eds). *The Wisdom of Ethel Percy Andrus.*
    Long Beach, California: NRTA/AARP 1968.
Hiltner, Seward. "Religion and the Aging Process," in Tibbitts, Clark
    (ed.) *Handbook of Social Gerontology.* Chicago: University of
    Chicago Press, 1960.
Howe, Reuel L. *How to Stay Younger While Growing Older.* Waco,
    Texas: Word Books, 1974.
Maslow, Abraham H. *Toward a Psychology of Being.* New York: D.
    Nostrand Co., 1968.
Maves, Paul B. "Aging, Religion and the Church," in Tibbitts, Clark
    (ed.). *Handbook of Social Gerontology.* Chicago: University of
    Chicago Press, 1960.
Maxwell, Jean M. *Center for Older People.* The National Council on the
    Aging. Washington, D.C. 1962.
The Church and the Older Kansan. Division of Services for the Aging,
    Kansas State Department of Social Welfare, 1968.
Tournier, Paul, M.D. *Learn To Grow Old.* New York: Harper and Row,
    1972.

4 Breaking The Ground

"What shall we do?" is the spoken or silent question in the minds and hearts of many people in the Judeo-Christian community when faced with the issue of ministry and older persons. Behind the question often lurks guilt, apathy, fear, frustration, and perhaps even quiet despair. Clear answers have not been coming. But some believe that hope is on the way. The story of Chatsworth Adult Center, San Diego, California, is one example of attempts being made to break the ground and claim the frontier.

CHATSWORTH ADULT CENTER

The beginning of the Chatsworth Adult Center coincided with the beginning of interest in programs for older persons in the Point Loma Community Presbyterian Church, San Diego, California. At the author's invitation, and with the support of the church officers and staff, an Older Adults Committee composed of seven members of the church was chosen and held its first meeting January 8, 1974, under his leadership. The Committee included three older couples and one young woman with some academic background in gerontology.

The Committee reviewed the church rolls and found that more than 400 persons, out of a total membership of approximately 2,000, were over 60 years of age. Another 400 were estimated to be between 50 and 60 years old. It was concluded that little was being done in the church and community, except for pastoral care being given by members of the church staff. A list of possible needs was made through sharing of experiences, including such concerns as survival, safety, social, self-esteem, and spiritual necessities. The Committee determined to work toward developing a program for and with older members of the church and community which could lead to meeting some of these needs. The stance was one of openness and learning. It was a wholly new experience for the Committee, as well as for the minister.

The first meeting of older persons was scheduled for Coffee and Fellowship on April 19, 1974. Approximately 40, or 10 percent of the 400 older members of the church attended. Interest was genuine and the desire to continue was strong enough to encourage the Committee to further exploration and activity. It was decided to meet monthly for an all-day program of singing, fellowship, and sack lunch, with special emphasis focused on one of the felt needs.

Out of the first meeting came an enlargement of the Older Adults Committee, thereafter called the Steering Committee, increasing the number to a total of 14, plus the minister as advisor. The new group continued to meet weekly, and began to seek the guidance of the Department on Aging, Catholic Community Services, Diocese of San Diego, and Senior Adult Services, San Diego. The group became aware of the Senior Centers in San Diego jointly sponsored by the Adult Education Department of San Diego Community Colleges, and Catholic Community Services.

TWELVE REJUVENATING TECHNIQUES

While pursuing studies toward the Doctor of Ministry degree at San Francisco Theological Seminary, I determined to work in the area of what churches can do toward helping older persons find renewal and fulfillment. In a summer academic session (1974), I discovered the Dissertation/ Project of Kenneth P. Berg (1974). In this work Dr. Berg revealed Twelve Rejuvenating Techniques which he believed to be of positive help to older persons. I determined to make the techniques operational in a setting where they could be experienced and tested.

When I returned from the Seminary, the group of older people were found to be ready to consider moving from a local church expression of concern for meeting needs of older persons to a wider usefulness which could be accomplished through becoming one of the Senior Centers sponsored by the Adult Education Department of San Diego Community Colleges and Catholic Community Services. After careful discussion the decision was made, and on October 8, 1974 it became the sixth in a series of such centers in metropolitan San Diego. The new arrangement provided for a paid "Coordinator," responsible both to the Community Colleges and Catholic Community Services. Because of my interest in the direction of the Center, it was agreed that I would be given authority for program leadership to enhance what was felt to be the uniqueness of the Center.

It is believed this arrangement has worked to benefit the Center and allowed the possibility of conducting the Action/Investigation Project as hoped for, providing a learning experience for all concerned. Since that date, weekly meetings have been held on Tuesdays from 9:00 a.m. to 3:00 p.m. The name Chatsworth Senior Center, chosen by the group at its initial meeting, was later changed by them to Chatsworth Adult Center. It was felt that the program and opportunity for growth would appeal to *all* adults. The significance of the name "Chatsworth" is that the church is located on Chatsworth Boulevard. Members of the group chose that in preference to identifying it with the name of the church on whose premises it meets. The Center has become a place for any and all who wish to attend, and thus is a genuine community and ecumenical resource. Its by-laws state: "It shall be an outreach ministry of Point Loma Community Presbyterian Church and affiliated with Catholic Community Services and San Diego Community Colleges."

As to purpose they declare: "The purpose of the Center shall be to provide an opportunity and a place for its members to meet to socialize, to learn, to grow; and in Christian fellowship, through sharing, to discover and employ the resources of older people in meeting their own needs and the needs of older persons in the community, thus promoting renewal and fulfillment."

ACTION/INVESTIGATION PROJECT

The idea of using the Twelve Rejuvenating Techniques as the primary educational focus of program emphasis was introduced to the Steering Committee. The request was made to test these techniques in an Action/Investigation Project, although the concept was new and strange. The acceptance came slowly as they were encouraged to move ahead in the spirit of adventure for growth. As the months passed, the Committee made an unbelievable investment of time and ·energy in the project. Without their interest and cooperation, coupled with the patience and persistence of the investigator, the project could not have been undertaken, much less completed.

In order for the Committee to understand the meaning of the Twelve Rejuvenating Techniques, a small group read Berg's Dissertation/Project with the purpose of defining the techniques for possible programmatic use. It seemed wise to consult specialists in gerontology, inviting them to respond to the redefinitions of the Twelve Techniques as foundations for testing in a Center for older persons. Several such persons were thus involved. Their responses ranged from critical questioning of the validity, adequacy, completeness, and usefulness of the Techniques as a constellation for renewal and fulfillment of older persons, to encouragement in using them as a resource for further study of older persons and to add to the literature through a report of the proposed project.

The investigator turned to Carol Clark, wife of the Head of Staff of Point Loma Community Presbyterian Church, asking her to do a "mouse story" on the Twelve Rejuvenating Techniques. Mrs. Clark, a gifted photographer and creator of audio-visual stories for children, uses miniature felt mice made by the women of the Martha Circle of the church, as characters for her productions. The result of her effort is an audio-visual, "The Second Spring of Samantha Muffin," which is proving to be a positive contribution to raising consciousness about the needs and possibilities of older persons as they seek renewal and fulfillment.

The audio-visual was devised as a basic interpretive tool to assist members of the Center in understanding the concepts of the Twelve Rejuvenating Techniques, and to help prepare them for participating with meaning in the Action/Investigation Project. It was introduced to the Center April 1, 1975. The response was enthusiastic! News of "The Second Spring of Samantha Muffin" spread quickly. The audio-visual has been produced as a film-strip and is available through United Presbyterian Health Education and Welfare Department of the United Presbyterian Church in the U.S.A., together with a Study Guide which I prepared.

The project was lengthened to a period of ten months. The Steering Committee assumed responsibility for developing and conducting programs for experiencing and testing the Twelve Rejuvenating Techniques. The process included these: (1) assignment of separate committees to deal with each Technique; (2) approval of programs submitted to the Steering Committee; (3) approval of programs submitted to the investigator's advisor at the Ethel Percy Andrus Gerontology Center, University of Southern California (Los Angeles); (4) presentation of programs to members of the Center; (5) Pre and Post Self-Rating Tests related to each Technique; and (6) evaluation of responses in a written report by the investigator. A complete account of the process, including programs and testing forms, may be found in the investigator's Dissertation/Project.

For the purpose of brevity in this chapter, I am showing only the Redefinitions of the Twelve Rejuvenating Techniques and broad brush results of the comprehensive test related to all Twelve Techniques.

1. **Remotivation**
   Apathy in older persons, often produced by isolation and loneliness, tends to cause them to replace persons and relationships with objects, and thus to lose alertness.

Remotivation can be encouraged through the sharing of personal history, significant events, and common experiences. Relationships are discovered, established, and maintained through sharing which can lead to further personal growth and involvement in society.

2. **Physical Conditioning**
Physical conditioning through adequate and regular exercise is basic to a sense of well-being. Older persons need assistance in discovering the kinds of exercise appealing and appropriate to them, and motivation to assure their use of such exercise.

3. **Education**
Personal growth is a life-long need and process. Older persons retain the ability to learn. The elderly need to be made aware of and encouraged to use the multiple opportunities for adult education in their communities. The possibilities range from such general types of improvement as completing a high school course for a diploma, learning new skills, teaching others, and courses for the sheer joy of learning. A few known needs are financial education, nutrition, and health and safety issues.

4. **Creative Resiliency**
A positive mental attitude is basic to a satisfying life. It helps persons in becoming resilient, enabling them to rebound from loss or defeat.

5. **Identification**
The will to live is essential to a full life. While accepting the fact of aging, people need to be introduced to examples of older persons who are living life to the fullest by identifying with the spirit of life and power rather than of weakness.

6. **Acclimation to Death**
The issue of death and dying confronts every person and is especially real to the elderly. The church is uniquely equipped and called to assist them in openly facing this reality so that they can be free to live creatively, confident that the promises of God about life now and beyond death are supportive and dynamic, and can help

them live with courage and meaning, and die with dignity and assurance.

7. **Leisure Ethic**

   Older persons need help both in accepting their leisure without guilt and in creatively using it. Giving of the self for the well-being of others is a sign of fulfillment and the affirmation of life.

8. **Spiritual Renewal**

   Spiritual renewal is essential to life fulfillment. The church has a special call to work with older persons toward this goal for their lives, recognizing the unlimited resources of the Christian faith for making life new. The strengthening of personal faith is a primary mission for the church and needs to be pursued with sensitivity, imagination, creativity, and persistence.

9. **Community**

   Self-worth is closely related to a sense of independence, which is a prized possession of every person. In the face of loss and change, older persons need reinforcement and assistance in maintaining their independence. Taking responsibility for their own lives through planning, creating, conducting, and participating in activities for themselves and others is basic to achieving and maintaining independence. The leadership potential in older persons is powerful and promising although largely unappreciated and untapped, and must be acknowledged and employed.

10. **Pre-Retirement Counseling**

    Retirement is one of the major transitions of life and is often traumatic. Preparation for this event encompassing the needs of the whole person is highly important and often makes the difference between successful retirement and the downhill slide into nothingness. Ideally, such counseling should begin as early as age 35. The need to retire *to* something, not *from* something is gaining acceptance.

11. **United Action**

    The needs, problems, and possibilities of the aging are not limited to any one cultural, ethnic, economic, or religious group. Ecumenical and secular agencies can and must work together to create a positive impact in meeting the common needs of older people to make aging a vital experience.

12. **Senior Power**
    Older persons are a vast national resource and are best equipped to take initiative for improving the image and conditions of life for senior citizens through action in political involvement. The church needs to encourage older persons to reach beyond themselves and lead in creating meaningful social roles for the elderly.

COMPREHENSIVE TEST FINDINGS

The investigator sought to determine the influence of the Twelve Rejuvenating Techniques in the lives of participants in the Center through a comprehensive test given on November 25, 1975, at the conclusion of programs on all Twelve Techniques. Respondents engaged in self-rating by *Looking Back* (How I would rate myself when I first learned of 12 Rejuvenating Techniques, Samantha Muffin, 3/11/75) and *Now* (How I rate myself, November 25, 1975).

(See Table I.)

For the purpose of this book, the following changes are noted as significant:

1. Ratings in *highs* had *increased* in each technique, some dramatically:

Remotivation	460%
Physical Conditioning	150%
Education	375%
Creative Resiliency	162%
Identification	136%
Acclimation to Death	41%
Leisure Ethic	69%
Spiritual Renewal	92%
Community	120%
Pre-Retirement Counseling	55%
United Action	133%
Senior Power	64%

Table I. Change in Self Rating in 12 Areas of Concern as a Result of Studying the Rejuvenating Techniques (numbers indicate actual responses)

CONCERNS	LOOKING BACK (N=50) How I would rate myself when I first learned of 12 Rejuvenating Techniques (Samantha Muffin 3/11/75)				NOW (N=50) How I rate myself November 25, 1975			
	High	Average	Low	No Response	High	Average	Low	No Response
Remotivation	5	33	6	6	28	16	0	6
Physical conditioning	8	28	8	6	20	24	4	2
Education	4	38	3	5	19	25	2	4
Creative resiliency	8	24	12	6	21	25	2	2
Identification	11	21	8	10	26	16	0	8
Acclimation to death	17	15	13	5	24	16	3	7
Leisure ethic	16	23	5	6	27	14	0	9
Spiritual Renewal	13	23	8	6	25	19	2	4
Community	10	26	8	6	22	23	1	4
Pre-retirement Counseling	9	19	14	8	14	23	5	8
United Action	6	25	10	9	14	27	2	7
Senior Power	14	16	13	7	23	21	0	6

2. Ratings in *lows* had *decreased* in each technique, some
   dramatically:

Remotivation	100%
Physical Conditioning	50%
Education	33%
Creative Resiliency	83%
Identification	100%
Acclimation to Death	77%
Leisure Ethic	100%
Spiritual Renewal	75%
Community	88%
Pre-Retirement Counseling	64%
United Action	80%
Senior Power	100%

An extended evaluation of the results of this test might
be useful in further research. However, the above are noted as
significant, recognizing that: (1) perhaps 75% of the
respondents had participated over the entire period of the
project; (2) not all had experienced every program or
technique; (3) respondents were attempting to recall and rate
themselves over a ten month period; (4) no one was required
to take the test.

Responses made in relation to Remotivation deserve
attention. The programs for Remotivation were not aimed at
persons in the Center, the Committee having decided that
people who attended were motivated and did not need
Remotivation. On the other hand, respondents to other
programs in the Center indicated their highest gain in
self-rating over the ten month period to be in Remotivation
(460%). It is apparent that experience in the Center increased
motivation of respondents to a very high degree, which was
perceived by them as *Remotivation.* A further interpretation
is that this means motivated people need continuing renewal
of their motivation.

Chatsworth Adult Center, having used the Twelve
Rejuvenating Techniques, believes they represent a holistic
approach to the needs of older persons, and therefore are
effective when used alone and together on a continuing basis.
Having finished the Action/Investigation Project, expressions
of leaders of the group have been that the Techniques will

continue to be held in the consciousness for program planning, guidance, development, and evaluation.

Average attendance at meetings of the Chatsworth Adult Center has increased from six to over 100 in the three years of its life. The greatest growth took place during the adventure of breaking the ground by putting the concepts of the Twelve Rejuvenating Techniques into operation.

The Center continues to emit rays of hope and signs of help for older persons, both in the church and in the community. The word has spread through its members that something unique and strong is under way, and that the door is open for any and *all* adults who wish to enter its life.

REFERENCES

Berg, Kenneth P. "The Church Responds to the Identity Crisis of the Aging," from *Senior Power: New Life for the Church,* a Dissertation Project presented to the Department of Advanced Pastoral Studies, San Francisco Theological Seminary, March 15, 1974.

5 Sowing The Seed

A stated intention of this book is to move from conceptualizing to actually providing practical, specific help for leaders in congregations. Most religious leaders will welcome information about programs which give evidence of the renewal and fulfillment of older persons. Such programs can be evaluated and compared by the reader. The hope is that from the samples offered, congregational leaders may find models which they can use in total or in part to stimulate their ministries among older persons. This book will become a working resource for local ministry in churches and synagogues.

Through an extended process of seeking information about positive models worthy of inclusion in this book, a number of possibilities were discovered, selected, and in some ways evaluated. From these, several have been selected for presentation here.

Letters were sent to representatives of 31 religious bodies, Protestant, Catholic, Eastern Orthodox, and Jewish, related to the National Interfaith Coalition on Aging. The request was for suggestions of models which might be included in this book. Similar letters were sent to secular sources such as the National Council on the Aging, Inc., American Association of Retired Persons, and National Retired Teachers Association. Many helpful responses were received. A list of all responses will be found in the Appendix.

Problems encountered in this effort included a lack of knowledge of specific programs by many denominational leaders, and a lack of specific evidence of renewal and fulfillment in local programs. In only one or two cases was there an indication that actual evaluation, through testing or opinion taking, had been sought; most suggested programs were bits and pieces of attempts to meet global needs of older persons. Only a few were multi-purpose in scope.

Criteria for selection of models for inclusion in this book include the number of recommendations for a single program; the nature, variety, scope, geographic location, reported effectiveness, and religious cross-section of programs; and the extent to which older persons themselves were involved in the developing and conducting of programs in which they participated.

The sample models chosen represent:

A large ecumenical Center in the mid-west

A program conducted by a single Protestant congregation in the mid-west

An ecumenical/secular sponsored Center on the West Coast in which a testing program was conducted

A Roman Catholic model in the East

A Jewish Community Center in the West

The largest independent program for older persons in America, with local, regional, and national impact

A typical secular Senior Center in a West Coast city

These models are presented here in detail:

MODEL NO. 1

The Shepherd's Center
5218 Oak Street
Kansas City, Missouri 64112

The Shepherd's Center is perhaps the most unique and promising model in the nation of a comprehensive multi-purpose center under religious auspices focused upon the renewing and fulfilling of older persons. The Shepherd's Center is an ecumenical project sponsored by 22 churches and synagogues. Its purpose is to help the elderly remain independent. For three years the Center was financed by the Department of Community Affairs, Office of Aging, and by private contributions. It is now totally community supported. A major program within the Center is the Mid-America Resource and Training Center on Aging, an outgrowth of the Shepherd's Center, created to provide resources in the field of aging.

Concept of the Center. Under the leadership of Rev. Elbert C. Cole, a study was conducted to determine the greatest needs of the community. It had been assumed that retirement housing was the most urgent need. Results showed that top priority was the creation of a community service group capable of helping older people remain in their own homes. The Sherphered's Center was developed in the summer of 1972 to meet this need. The name was chosen because of its image of a caring network capable of sustaining people on a short- or long-term basis.

It became evident that the needs of the target area, 53,000 persons, 11,603 over age sixty-five, required the combined efforts of as many congregations as possible. The project became an ecumenical effort with twenty-two churches and synagogues uniting to design services needed for survival, using older persons themselves as planners and volunteers. It is estimated that the Center is now reaching one out of every four elderly persons in the target community. The Shepherd's Center is incorporated with a board of directors of twenty-four community residents, many of them elderly. It serves as a channel for any agency or service in Metropolitan Kansas City available to older people in the target area.

Objectives of the Center.

To sustain the desire for independence, characteristic of most elderly people.

To offer an integrative approach in meeting individual needs by bringing a wide variety of services from one center.

To focus on the elderly of a specific geographical area, small enough to accomplish the goals of the Center.

To provide opportunities for the elderly to serve and engage in meaningful activities.

To avoid isolating the elderly from the rest of the community.

To develop a model which could be duplicated elsewhere in the city and in other communities.

To make more effective use of existing community resources and programs designed to help those 65 and over.

Heavy reliance on volunteers to accomplish the objectives of the Center.

Keep the elderly in the mainstream of life (viable alternative to institutional care).

Challenge assumptions about the elderly by providing a clinical situation for effective research.

Experiment and pioneer in new services.

Program of the Center. The program of the Center is two-fold, involving over 250 organized volunteers (98% over 65) to offer both home services and center activities.

Home Services: There are nine basic areas of service, all formulated to help people remain in their own homes:

1. **Meals on Wheels**
   Nearly 50 retired male volunteers deliver a hot noon-time meal five days a week to 55-60 home-bound people or to people temporarily limited after hospitalization or during an illness. Special diets are available when ordered by a physician. The food is prepared at the Swope Ridge Health Care Center.

2. **Shoppers**
   Older recipients in the target area, unable to shop for themselves, are taken to the markets and other stores by

older volunteers. In some cases, shopping is done for recipients.

3. **Wheels that Care**
   Volunteer drivers, using their own cars, provide transportation to meet critical needs such as medical appointments or other emergency or essential situations for about 20 to 30 people.

4. **Handyman**
   Approximately 30 retired, skilled workmen make small repairs, such as electrical, minor plumbing, and carpentry — even painting — for a small fee. Fees are paid directly to the handyman. Recipients are limited to elderly target areas residents. About 100 residents are served each month.

5. **Friendly Visitors**
   About 20 home-bound people receive regular visits and telephone calls from individual and community groups. The Soroptomist Club assigns volunteers.

6. **Companion Aides**
   Help with meals, housekeeping, and other chores is available through the companion aide service. Rates are negotiable and are paid to the employee.

7. **Security and Protection**
   Trained crime prevention aides, all volunteers over 65, assist victims in obtaining whatever assistance is needed. They deal with resolving anxiety, prevention measures, safety instruction, and other means of helping older persons. The volunteers are trained and supervised by the Midwest Research Institute and the Kansas City Police Department.

8. **Care Twenty**
   Free meals with homemaker services are available to persons with limited incomes.

9. **Night Team**
   The Shepherd's Center keeps in touch with people through a 24-hour answering service with a night team of clergymen responding to emergencies.

Center Activities. The other focus of the Shepherd's Center program is directed toward the "young elderly" who meet in the facilities of Central United Methodist Church. Several aspects are included:

Adventures in Learning: Every Friday, up to 40 classes and activities are offered by volunteer instructors in stimulating subjects to help older persons keep in the mainstream of life. Classes are held year-round in fall, winter, spring, and summer terms. People attend as many classes as they wish, selecting a class each hour at whatever time they arrive, from 8:00 A.M. to 3:00 P.M. *The Forum* at noon presents a varied program of community leaders on current topics. A hot lunch is served for $1.00. The registration fee is $4.00 per term. A Tuesday/Thursday schedule has also been added to accommodate arts and crafts specialties.

The Adventures in Learning model was borrowed from the St. Luke's School of Continuing Education program for older persons, initiated nearly fifteen years ago by Rev. Joseph T. Shackford, Director, St. Luke's United Methodist Church, Oklahoma City.

This model is recommended as basic to effective use of volunteers in continuing education sponsored by churches and synagogues, for the renewal and fulfillment of older persons.

The following is a typical term's program for Adventures in Learning courses and activities, planned in four categories for each hour:

1. **Head**
   Learning and Growth opportunities

2. **Heart**
   Emotional and spiritual input

3. **Hand**
   Arts and crafts

4. **Hind-end**
   Entertainment through travelogues, book reviews, etc.

Enrollment at the Shepherd's Center is between 600-800 each semester, with an average attendance every week of over 400.

Life Enrichment: This nine-week program brings together a limited number of older persons who need additional support, love, and understanding. It is for those whose physical, emotional, and spiritual resources have been depleted. In association with others in need and under professional guidance, the emphasis is on finding renewal and fulfillment. The Life Enrichment basic course meets once each week. The Life Enrichment advanced seminar, limited to former participants, also meets weekly. Membership cost for either class is $5.00.

Health Fair: An annual Health Fair is held each fall, providing lectures, exhibits, information, and tests — all free — for persons 60 years of age and older. Thirty-five to forty agencies provide the exhibits.

Health Screening: A public health nurse is available on Fridays at the Adventures in Learning program to consult with Center participants about health problems, blood pressure checks, etc.

Pre-Retirement Seminar: Offered annually, in six sessions to persons approaching retirement age, this is a series of lectures on problems which confront retirees. Admission is free.

Advocacy Role: The Center is continuously on the alert for opportunities to represent and/or support political processes related to the aging and the aged.

Mid-America Resource and Training Center on aging. An integral component of the Shepherd's Center, this resource coordinates existing agencies and individuals affiliated with geriatrics to provide consolidation of efforts to help older Americans achieve a more meaningful existence. The Center serves as a collection point of published materials on aging and its library houses audio-visuals as well as reference materials. Training courses are conducted for directors and workers in multi-purpose senior centers. Seminars are held for local agency staff and volunteers.

For further information write to:
The Shepherd's Center
5218 Oak Street
Kansas City, Missouri 64112
or

Mid-America Resource and Training Center on Aging
5218 Oak Street
Kansas City, Missouri 64112

MODEL NO. 2

Senior Adult Ministries

First Church of the Nazarene
Bethany, Oklahoma

The Senior Adult Ministry of the First Church of the Nazarene, Bethany, Oklahoma, is a sample of work among older persons conducted by a single Protestant congregation. The nature and program of this model will be found in *Senior Adult Ministries with Brother Sam* (1974), written by the Rev. Sam Stearman, Minister of Pastoral Care of the 2,000 member church.

Begun in 1972, this ministry is fourfold in which seniors:

1. Serve others
2. Do things for themselves
3. Are served by others
4. Experience a program designed for them.

The motto is: Fun living while growing older.

The ministry is aimed at persons 65 and older who are lonely, inactive, and may have lost the meaning of life.

The program is outlined under the above four categories.

SAM in Service (serving others). "Sunshine Sams" (Senior Adult Men), and "Sals" (Senior Adult Ladies), give of themselves to fulfill social and fellowship needs in nursing care homes and to shut-ins. This ministry reaches not only the persons in need, but their families as well.

"Helping Hannahs and Homers" supervise the "Church Pantry" and the distribution of food, clothing, and furniture when need arises. The Church Pantry is resupplied by members of the congregation at Thanksgiving. Hannahs and

Homers give emergency financial help on a non-continuing basis, a maximum of $10.00 in urgent situations. The fund is maintained by mid-week offerings. Medicine, furniture, and clothing are supplied according to need.

"Hallelujah Hatties and Henry's" focus attention on the spiritual needs of shut-ins and the disabled. Among their activities are: helping shut-ins write letters; reading aloud to them; giving manicures; holding weekly morning Bible classes in the home of a member unable to attend church; encouraging participation of shut-ins by addressing mailings for the church and keeping attendance records up to date; providing large-print Bibles and devotional literature; encouraging shut-ins to plan their own social events; and remembering birthdays and anniversaries.

"SAM in Action" (doing things for themselves). This program includes singing groups, puppet shows, soloists; sack lunch ("Come with lunch in one hand and a friend in the other."); arts and crafts. The fee is approximately $2.00 per semester for supplies. A different project is undertaken each time with younger persons as instructors.

Sacred Order of the Golden Spoke. Older persons use adult tricycles for exercise, shopping, and local transportation. Vehicles are specially tagged with a medallion.

Shoppers Bus. The church bus is used bimonthly for trips to shopping centers or to art museums, etc., in the morning, returning to the activity center for afternoon programs.

Armchair Travelog. Whan a tour is being planned, films are shown relating to the itinerary, followed by arts and crafts during the first Tuesday of the month program.

Ping Pong, Caroms and Forty-Two. Periodic evening meetings are held from 7:00 to 9:00 for games (dominoes, shuffleboard, ping pong, etc.). Refreshments follow, and information is shared about sick persons, persons with special needs. The meeting concludes with prayer.

"SAM being Served" (being served by others). An annual Valentine Sweetheart Banquet is sponsored by senior women of Bethany Nazarene College across the street from the church. The Banquet is for older couples, singles, and their escorts. College students decorate and serve in the program that follows.

Christmas Banquet. Another intergenerational experience is sponsored by junior high young people and is held for senior adults. Young people raise money from projects. Mothers of teenagers plan the menu and prepare the food. Two or three adults are assigned to each junior high young person. Each senior adult is invited and escorted by a youth to a noon-time banquet on a Saturday before Christmas. Fathers provide transportation. Young people eat with the persons they have escorted. Santa Claus appears with peppermint candy for all. Special gifts are given for the oldest, the couple married longest, ones with the most children, etc.

Circle K Chore Company. College young men give service to senior adults by doing odd jobs without pay. They spade flower beds, remove tree stumps, unplug downspouts, etc. Calls are made to the church office. A representative of CCC picks up the calls and makes assignments. A contribution may be made to Circle K's multiple sclerosis projects.

"Program for SAM" (special programs). The Perfume Brigade is important to SAM programs. Brother Sam says, "When a beautiful, well-groomed, perfume-laden younger lady steps into the midst of my people — whether it is a hostess on a bus trip or as an instructor of arts and crafts — my senior adults come alive. (And not just the men!) A wise leader will stuff his volunteer staff with as much of the 'perfume set' as is available. Older people seem to see in that young lady their own daughter or granddaughter." These younger women help with crafts, make coffee, do set-up for meetings, manage the kitchen for luncheons, and serve as hostesses on bus tours.

Bethany Place. Bethany Place is a church-sponsored 72-room apartment complex for older persons. It is low cost housing.

Travel. The one activity that has surpassed all others in excitement and participation is the travel tours.

Minor Tours, i.e., Annual Azalea Tour in the spring and Foliage Tour in the fall (one day and four states), are popular.

Major tours are scheduled once every six months. Trips last from one day to two weeks, cover a few miles or as much as 5,000 miles. Tours are planned to be memorable experiences. Featured are daily devotionals on the bus(es) using cassette tapes for music and sing-a-longs, scripture and message. Emphasis is on first class accommodations, advanced planning, and reservations.

For further information write to:

Senior Adult Ministries
First Church of the Nazarene
6749 N.W. 39th Expressway
Bethany, Oklahoma 73008

MODEL NO. 3

Chatsworth Adult Center

Point Loma Community Presbyterian Church
San Diego, California

The Chatsworth Adult Center meets under ecumenical and secular auspices. It is one of twelve Senior Centers sponsored by Catholic Community Services Department of Aging and San Diego Community Colleges. All but four of the centers meet in church facilities. Point Loma Community Presbyterian Church, San Diego, California, provides both the facilities and most of the membership of the Chatsworth Adult Center.

Organization and Attendance. The Center has been in operation for more than three years, growing from an average weekly attendance of six to over 100. It meets each week of the year on Tuesdays (except holidays) from 9:00 A.M. to 3:00 P.M., and is developing into a multi-purpose facility. The community colleges provide a coordinator and two aides. There is no charge for attendees.

A Board of Directors, elected by the membership, has begun leadership following completion of the leadership by the Steering Committee. By-laws have been drafted and distributed.

Major Features. Major features of the Center include high level participation on the part of members in the development and conduct of the entire program; personal and group sharing of needs, experiences, and growth opportunities; informal singing and celebration of birthdays and anniversaries; stimulating programs on a wide variety of subjects and issues of concern to older persons; classes led by volunteers in the membership and from the community; sack lunch with cookies supplied at each meeting; monthly potluck lunches; and pie and ice cream day, each once a month. Coffee is available throughout the day, the kitchen being handled by volunteers. "Chatsworth Chatter," a monthly newsletter has been inaugurated. In an effort to reach out to the community, interest is being shown in Meals on Wheels, Handyman Service, and Visitation.

Talent Bank. One of the outcomes of the action/ investigation project was the development of a Talent Bank of interests and skills of members. The Talent Bank is a ready resource for volunteer participation and future program development.

Five Major Concerns. Five major concerns of members of the Center were developed through participation in the "Delphi Process" of gathering data. Members came to the agreement that their mutual concerns are: entertainment; outreach; health concerns; general assistance to members; and senior power, in that order. The concerns, together with the Twelve Rejuvenating Techniques (see Chapter 4), set the tone and direction for the Center's life.

Structure of the Center

Board of Directors, consisting of:

    President

    Vice-President for Inreach Activities (Tuesday programs)

    Vice-President for Outreach Activities (service in the community)

    Secretary

    Treasurer

    Four persons elected by the membership

Advisor from the church staff
Adult school coordinator
Representative from Catholic Community Services

Inreach Activity Committees

Desk Committee — Greeters, Bulletin Board, Roster, Name Tags, Birthdays/Anniversary Dates, Information about illnesses

Telephone Committee — Calling absentees, liaison between desk, President, and Vice-President for Outreach; Telephone Reassurance

Classes and Activities Committee — Initiation, scheduling and coordination of classes, including leaders, classrooms, etc., recommended to Board of Directors for approval or change

Forum Program — Entertainment or speakers, approved by Board of Directors upon recommendation of the Coordinator

Bus Tours Committee — Initiation, scheduling, planning, and conducting of bus tours approved by Board of Directors

Kitchen Committee — Responsible for special day, i.e., Pie, Ice Cream, Birthdays, Anniversaries, Potlucks, ordering supplies, clean-up

House Committee — Setting up and cleaning of meeting room each week

Librarian — Stimulates interest in Church Library, and acts as liaison with Church Librarian

Outreach Activity Committees

Transportation Committee — Arranges for pick up and return to home on request of member or older person in the community

Handyman Service Committee — Provides handyman service by appointment for a nominal fee

Meals on Wheels — Provides meals by contract for persons unable to prepare their own food. Center representatives work with Meals on Wheels Committee for Point Loma/Ocean Beach area

Chatsworth Adult Center Interpretation Committee — Provides interpretation of Center organization and activities for individuals and groups interested in developing ministries among older persons

Visitation Committee — Coordinates visits to older persons in private homes, hospitals, residential care homes, and convalescent homes

Intergenerational Planning Committee — Seeks opportunities to meet and work with other age groups in the church and community

Legislative Concerns and Community Action Committee — Studies and recommends assistance in matters related to consumer fraud. Maintains contact with groups in community and the city of San Diego, seeking to improve the well-being of older persons, and initiates such action where appropriate. Studies and recommends action on legislation concerning the well-being of older persons

Community Resource (Information and Referral) — At least one person who is able to provide assistance to members in meeting various needs

Hospice — Representative on a San Diego ecumenical committee to develop a Hospice for the terminally ill

Publicity and Newsletter — Committee responsible for creating and publishing "Chatsworth Chatter," Center newsletter on a monthly basis, and for communicating news to local news media

Counseling — Interprets counseling resources available such as Point Loma Counseling Service, Inc., etc.

Chatsworth Adult Center changed its name from *Senior* to *Adult* when it recognized its importance to adults other than seniors. The meetings are open to adults of *all* ages, even though most of those who attend are 60 years of age and older.

The Center is committed to the renewal and fulfillment of older persons through a wide variety of opportunities, emphasizing the importance and involvement of each person in the leadership and conduct of the Center.

For further information write to:
Chatsworth Adult Center
2128 Chatsworth Blvd.
San Diego, California 92107

MODEL NO. 4

Project: HEAD Helping Elderly Adults Direct

Project HEAD was initiated and developed by Mrs. Victorina Peralta in 1974 when she served as Administrator, Department of Community Services on Aging, Catholic Social Services, Archdiocese of Philadelphia. She was also a Board member of the National Interfaith Coalition on Aging.

Project HEAD touches 165 parishes and 35,000 senior citizens in the Archdiocese of Philadelphia, but has spread to other religious bodies, communities, and states. It is designed for interfaith use and can be adapted as a model by congregations of many denominations

Background and Direction. Project HEAD is a way of organizing senior citizen groups within church settings in order to help them help themselves to improve the quality of life both for older persons and for society as a whole. The philosophy is based on the conviction that churches have the responsibility to provide ways in which obstacles to self-realization of older persons can be overcome or prevented. The goal is to encourage self-help and independent living so that older persons can continue in the mainstream of life and in their churches. The objective is to create a place of human dignity and worth in the community in matters that relate to finances, social contact and status, family bonds, and emotional and spiritual well-being. The purpose is to seek and strengthen the potential of the elderly.

Six Step Organization of Project HEAD

1. **Locate and Identify**
   Potential leaders among the aged in a given community are located and identified through their response to attractive posters placed in strategic places, i.e., stores, churches, bus stops, barbershops, etc. Announcements are made from altar or pulpit for three consecutive Sundays or sabbath days. Press releases are placed through neighborhood newspapers, radio, television, etc.

2. **Organize**
   A meeting of those responding to these invitations is set up immediately after the third Sunday or sabbath. The

goals, objectives, philosophy, and purpose of Project HEAD are explained, using human interest examples.

3. **Deputize**

   Temporary officers are appointed: President, Vice-President, Secretary, Treasurer, Membership Chairperson, Program Chairperson, Sunshine Chairperson, and chairpersons for each of the six-point programs. They continue in office for three months, after which time an election is held. Appointments are made on the basis of personality, commitment, and previous work experience.

4. **Supervise**

   Guidance is given for groups to grow and develop in their relationship with one another using the six-point program as a tool.

5. **Recognize**

   Recognition is given to the organization by issuing a charter as soon as the group is self-functioning.

6. **Continuous Evaluation of Progress.**

   Evaluation is conducted through mutual sharing conferences with staff, and in club meetings, regional meetings, and Council general meetings.

Six Point Program of Project HEAD

The program seeks to serve the whole person, and is comprehensive, with total spiritual well-being as its purpose.

1. **Social**

   Emphasis is on persons as social beings, needing companionship. Opportunities are given to build new friendships and social relationships to compensate for losses by death of loved ones, friends, and neighbors.

   Examples: Birthday parties, anniversaries, potluck suppers, holiday get-togethers, Telecare, dance parties.

2. **Health and Welfare**

   Maintenance of physical, mental, and spiritual health is the goal. Seminars, body dynamics, physical fitness programs, Sunshine committees, food stamps, Telecare, health fairs, nutritional classes, study clubs, health forums, volunteers visiting sick and shut-ins, and writing letters are all means of expressing and experiencing this area of concern.

3. **Education**

Emphasis is on challenging older persons to acquire new experiences through learning.

Examples: Book reviews, discussion groups, creative writing, educational tours, current events, spiritual retreats, Days of Recollection, Block Rosary, or devotional groups, Bible study groups, poetry clubs, trips, seminars, conferences, stamp collections.

4. **Cultural**

The purpose is to encourage appreciation of the cultural aspects of life by opening doors leading to cultural experience.

Examples: Musical concerts, cultural tours and trips, musical teas, plays, glee clubs, drama groups, choral groups, role play, etc. Encouragement of participation is made through performance in plays, musicals for the sick, or other senior centers. Formation of glee clubs, kitchen bands, drama groups is suggested.

5. **Leisure Time Recreation**

The focus is on the wise use of leisure, recognizing the importance of time in the later years of life. Trips, dancing, group singing, arts and crafts, ceramics, painting, card playing, volunteer work, traveling, tours, games are used.

6. **Civic Action**

Older people are encouraged to assume positive involvement in civic and non-partisan political concerns, to improve the image and condition of the aging and aged and of society in general. Persons are encouraged to work together for better income, better housing, better health care, better transportation. Care is taken that seniors are not taken advantage of by unscrupulous persons.

Examples: Lobbying for bills and legislation that will affect their welfare and the whole society. Letter writing and advocacy are encouraged.

The six-point emphasis is to provide multiple opportunities for actively involving persons in doing what they desire and choose to do.

The priest, rabbi, or pastor needs to play a triple role: as a motivator, enabler, and facilitator. The aged become effective partners and are able to serve the unreached and hard to reach elderly in their own community within the church or synagogue setting.

For further information write to:

Director of Community Services on Aging
Catholic Social Services
222 North 17th Street
Philadelphia, Pennsylvania 19103

MODEL NO. 5

Westside Jewish Community Center
Los Angeles, California

The Westside Jewish Community Center, the largest of six Centers in metropolitan Los Angeles serving one-half million Jews, is a notable example of work done among this segment of American life. The Center is part of the Jewish Centers Association.

General Background. Built in 1954, the Westside Jewish Community Center is a multi-purpose facility serving persons of all ages. Fifteen program staff members plan and supervise activities for 4,500 members. Another significantly large group of non-members avail themselves of the excellent equipment and programs. Programs are scheduled for Juniors (birth to 11 years of age), Teens (9th to 12th grades), Adults, and Senior Adults (65 years of age and older). The Center is open Monday through Friday from 9:00 A.M. to 11:00 P.M. Multiple use compels careful scheduling for each age group. The pool is open seven days a week. Some light programming in certain areas is scheduled on Sundays.

Annual membership dues are on a graded scale and are related to either: General Program or Health Club categories.

Fees for Senior Adults are $45.00 per year per person, or $65 per year per couple. Most parts of the program are covered by the Membership fee. Some classes charge a small fee (25 cents to 50 cents) per session. Non-members pay small, but somewhat larger fees for some parts of the program.

Senior Adult Program. The Senior Adult Program serves approximately 1,000 members, of whom about 500 are enrolled in classes. Other members and non-members participate in non-enrolled programs. Events are planned Monday through Friday, 9:00 A.M. to 3:00 P.M. A special religious/cultural program, Oneg Shabbat (Joy of Sabbath) is scheduled from 2:45 to 4:00 each Friday. Candlelighting, Yiddish, songs, and wine combine to help older Jews, 90 percent of whom are emigrants from Eastern Europe, welcome the Sabbath. Oneg Shabbat is planned and conducted by members of the Center.

Program emphases are in physical education, educational classes, and cultural/religious tradition. Most members attend two or more days each week, finding fellowship, inspiration, growth, and fun as they come from their places of living.

Scheduled throughout the days of the week are such opportunities as:

Folk Dancing
Politics and You
Drawing and Painting
Yiddish Literary Forum
Ceramics
Lip Reading
Body Dynamics
English Classes
English and Yiddish Drama Group
Creative Writing
Psychology
Personal History Group
Yiddish Poetry and Reading
Westside Symphonette
Chorus
Friendship Club

American Jewish History
Gerontology
Bridge
Piano
World Literature
Mt. Sinai Group (rehabilitation)
Oneg Shabbat
Jewish Blind
Trips
Kosher Meal (served five days a week for 100 persons at
    60 cents per plate).

Leadership and Service. Primary leadership of the Senior Adult Program is through paid Center Staff. Some classes are conducted by faculty from Los Angeles Board of Education Adult Schools. Some courses are taught by volunteers. The Symphonette, and Chorus of nearly 100, present periodic concerts for the larger community. Some members share in a "Buddy System" of telephone reassurance. Many strong friendships are developed and maintained among the people.

While the program appears to be largely designed for older persons rather than by them, a Senior Adult Program Board of Directors meets every Monday to give guidance to the program and staff.

There is a strong, positive cultural and historical emphasis within the Center for all ages. All are committed to Jewish life and tradition. Special emphasis is placed on Jewish holy days and holidays.

Funding. The Center is funded from three major sources: the United Jewish Welfare Fund, Membership Fees, and special fund-raising projects.

For further information write to:

The Westside Jewish Community Center
5870 W. Olympic Blvd.
Los Angeles, California 90036

MODEL NO. 6

AARP/NRTA

American Association of Retired Persons and
National Retired Teachers Association

The American Association of Retired Persons and the National Retired Teachers Association are national organizations committed to overcoming the neglect and deprivation of older persons by "improving the quality of life for older Americans."

Both organizations have the same founder, Dr. Ethel Percy Andrus. Both function on the local, state, and national levels under carefully structured policies and procedures. AARP and NRTA are the largest independent organizations of older persons in the nation. The benefits, programs, and effectiveness of AARP/NRTA, largely through legislative effort, are remarkable.

Interviews were held with four persons closely related to AARP/NRTA: Mrs. Ruth Lana, Honorary President of AARP, and Coordinator of AARP Travel Services; Miss Dorothy Crippen, Historian, Director of Publications and Membership Processing, and President-Chairman, Institute of Lifetime Learning, AARP/NRTA; Fred H. Dewey, Regional Representative, Area IX, NRTA/AARP; and Edward G. Schumm, Assistant Regional Representative, District IX, NRTA/AARP.

History. The National Retired Teachers Association was founded by Dr. Ethel Percy Andrus in 1947 following her distinguished career as an educator. It grew out of her concern for the well-being of retired teachers, many of whom were suffering multiple social, status, and financial losses. Members of families of NRTA requested similar benefits for other retired persons. AARP was organized in 1958 in response to that need. These two bodies, together with AIM (Action for Independent Maturity), now number over 8 million members. More than 2,400 chapters of AARP and units of NRTA serve and are served by older persons who belong to them. Those who knew Dr. Andrus best declare that she gave more to older people, and did more to help them improve their place in American life, than any other one person.

Membership in NRTA is open to all retired teachers and administrators. Annual membership dues are $2.00 per person, including subscriptions to *NRTA Journal* and the *NRTA News Bulletin.*

Membership in AARP is open to persons 55 years of age and older, retired or not. Membership dues are $3.00 per year or $5.00 for three years including subscriptions to *Modern Maturity* and the *AARP News Bulletin.*

Purpose. While the purpose of NRTA was related solely to the needs of the teaching community, and to retired teachers, through legislative action, a wider-scoped purpose marks all three groups at this time. The purpose is to help older persons meet their problems more realistically, more economically, and more successfully. The motto is, "to serve and not to be served."

AARP Chapters. AARP seeks to be a grass roots place where social benefits, community service, and social action can be furthered. Local chapters are organized under the national AARP policies. Details of how a chapter is formed may be found in *How to Organize an AARP Chapter.*

In addition to four prescribed officers, five standing committees are required: Nominating, Membership, Legislative, Program, and Publicity. Other committees may be formed. Dues range between $1.00 and $2.00 per year. Guidebooks are prepared for committee chairpersons. Workshops are conducted each year for officers and committee chairpersons. Chapters constitute only 10 percent of total AARP membership. They are service-oriented bodies with particular emphasis on legislation.

Legislative Division. Legislative involvement of members is urged at all levels. Each local chapter has a Legislative Committee. A Joint NRTA/AARP State Legislative Committee functions in every state. The National Legislative Council of 20 members functions on the national level. Specific, non-partisan recommendations are made at all levels to improve the lot of older Americans and of society as a whole. There are paid lobbyists. A paid research staff in

Washington, D.C. assists in developing legislation. Stated goals of the legislative division are: economic security, adequate health care facilities and services, adequate housing at affordable prices, improved transportation services, rejection of policies of age discrimination, and new social roles and employment of opportunities that will utilize the wisdom and experience of older persons.

The Institute of Lifetime Learning. The Institute of Lifetime Learning is an optional program. Chapters may elect to use this means for educational growth of its members under strictly adhered to guidelines. In May, 1975, there were over 30 extension Institutes of Lifetime Learning in various locations in the U.S. All are self-sustaining and locally administered. They offer short-term, non-graded courses under qualified teachers, selected by the local advisory committee. Most courses run from six to eight weeks, with a cost from free to $16.00 for each subject. Most institutes are set up cooperatively by NRTA and AARP members and colleges, universities, community groups, and other organizations, using community facilities. The organization manual is *Formula for Success.*

Services of AARP/NRTA. An extensive, useful cluster of services is offered to members of AARP/NRTA members:

Consumer Information Program
Publications
Health Education Program
Institute of Lifetime Learning
Tax-Aide Program
Legislative Role
Ethel Percy Andrus Gerontology Center
Travel Service
Courtesy discounts at leading hotels and auto rental companies
Vacation holidays (for groups)
Group Health Insurance Programs
Nursing Home Program (Ojai, California)
Home Delivery Pharmacy Service
Hospitality Lounges in four cities
Consulting Service for Local Chapters
Church Programs

Recommended Auto Insurance
Driver Improvement Program
Recommended Mature-Temps, Inc.
Senior Community Service Aides Project
Recommended Life Insurance
Crime Prevention Program

For further information write to:

National Retired Teachers Association
American Association of Retired Persons
1225 Connecticut Avenue, N.W.
Washington, D.C. 20036

MODEL NO. 7

Pasadena Senior Center
85 East Holly Street
Pasadena, California 91103

Pasadena Senior Center is included among the models of programs for renewing and fulfilling of older persons. It stands as an example of the several thousand secular senior centers in America.

Origin of the Center. The need for a Center for older persons in Pasadena has existed for many years. Population figures indicated rapid growth in the number of persons over 50 over an extended period of time. The Community Chest and Pasadena Welfare Council recommended creation of a Citizens' Committee to consider the needs of older persons in the community. A steering committee of 21 members led in the process to acquire property in Memorial Park, and in the development of facilities and programs to serve individuals and groups of older persons. Pasadena Senior Center, costing $152,000 was opened in May, 1960.

Membership and Finances. Persons over 50 years of age are eligible for membership. Dues are $5.00 per year. The Center is unique as a cooperative venture between the private and public sectors. The city of Pasadena owns the building located in the park, and contributes all maintenance and utilities, plus a cash amount towards the director's salary. The citizen Board of Directors raises funds for operating expenses through solicitation of friends. Members contribute nearly 30 percent of the operating budget by participating in center activities, paying dues, and sponsoring rummage sales and bazaars. A members' monthly meeting is held on the first Tuesday of every month (September-June) to discuss the business of the center. The meeting is preceded by a potluck luncheon and entertainment.

Classes, Programs, and Activities. Classes are conducted by the Adult Education Department of Pasadena City College and are scheduled to meet the needs and requests of the members. Programs vary with the wishes of the members. Monday card parties, variety programs, travelogues, bingo, a monthly birthday party, pancake breakfasts, potluck luncheons, and special holiday celebrations are held. "Musical Seniors" rehearse regularly and present programs at the Center and for retirement homes and hospitals. The Men's Club meets regularly. The Golden Age Dance Club holds dances every Thursday and Saturday afternoon. Professional musicians provide the music. Frequent, well-planned trips are scheduled. Outdoor activities include shuffleboard, ping-pong, cards, and chess. Community Helpers meet each week to sew and knit for persons in need.

Services. The Center offers minibus service, information and referral, tax assistance, and other services. Volunteers are sought to help in most programs and activities. A monthly newsletter is produced by the Center and mailed to subscribers for $1.25 per year. *News Vane* carries information about programs, classes, special events, activities, and other information, much of which is related to personal news. Want ads are welcome.

The Center is open Monday through Friday, 8:30 A.M. to 4:30 P.M.; Saturday and Sunday, 12 noon to 4:30 P.M.

Typical daily classes include lip reading, Spanish, drawing and painting, physical fitness, art of conversation, orchestra, challenge of maturity, needle arts, bazaar sewing, Musical Seniors, creative writing, focus on aging, bridge, ceramics, cards, travelogues.

Organization. Volunteers serve as officers and committee chairpersons for the Center. A staff of nine full- and part-time persons serve the Center.

For further information write to:

Pasadena Senior Center
85 East Holly Street
Pasadena, California 91103

MINI MODELS

In addition to the models which show a variety of programs to help older people meet their needs, three mini-models will be outlined. Each focuses on a specific type of concern. Included are a local church program using a simple means to serve the needs of neighbors, a mid-judicatory model of a Task Force on Older Adults, and a denominational series of annual retreats for older persons.

Local Church Program

"Bread Day"
First Lutheran Church, San Diego, California
For everyone Passing By Today
Come In and Share Bread
Hot Out of the Oven
and
Tea and Coffee
9 A.M. – 4 P.M.

This sign awaits passersby every Friday at the patio entrance of the First Lutheran Church, San Diego, California. The church building for this congregation numbering 380 members, 172 of whom are retired on fixed incomes, is relatively new. It replaced the old facility for a community of faith which refused to relocate in the suburbs, even though most of the members live in outlying areas.

Surrounding the church are businesses and apartment houses. A downtown hospital is nearby, as is a crash pad for transients with no place to sleep. Three mid-to-low cost high rise senior housing units, occupied by nearly 1000 older

persons, and sponsored by three different denominational
bodies, are within two blocks (one stands on the same
property as the church).

The Search for Contact. Under pastoral leadership, a
group sought for a way to make contact with unknown
neighbors in order to bear a witness to the Lord of life. The
goal was to find something to meet the needs of people, a
vehicle to draw others to the church facility for contact
where their needs could be met, and a bridge between the
scattered members and their downtown parish.

Among the brainstorming group was a social worker, the
wife of another Lutheran pastor. The idea of a Bread Day
came to her. She had talked to many persons of all ages and
backgrounds in the area. Why not make hot bread and invite
anyone and everyone to come and share it at no cost?

The group felt they had been led to the means of
making contact with the elderly, the business people, and the
transients and others, none of whom have anything in
common with the others except their humanity, personal
need, and a liking for hot fresh bread! Besides, bread has
great symbolic meaning for Christians.

The Bread, the Volunteers, and the Guests. The bread is
made in mini-tins, providing enough to make eight slices per
tin. Margarine is served separately in little paper cups. The
hot bread is taken from the oven, wrapped in foil, and served
at a table in the social hall. A hostess or two serves the bread,
tea and coffee, apple slices and cheese slices. A basket to
receive donations sits on the table.

Volunteers bake 48 loaves each week in the church
kitchen, in three batches, with about one-third left over for
freezing and reheating to begin serving the next Friday
morning. Baking begins about 8:30 A.M.

Card tables are set in the church patio and in the social
hall. Recorded music is played softly as background for
conversation and fellowship. A literature table carries a varied
assortment of pamphlets and other reading material. Brightly
colored banners hang from trees in the patio and on the walls
of the hall. The smell of hot bread permeates everything.

The volunteers are mostly members and friends of the
church who serve as hosts and hostesses. They welcome each

person who enters the patio and the hall. They join in conversation at the tables. The recipients of their friendly concern range in age up to 90 years old. Mornings tend to bring transients, while older people come in the afternoon.

The pastor and/or his staff assistant are present all day every Friday, listening, sharing, intervening where they can be of assistance. They offer a basic information and referral service to many who need specific help.

The guests find Bread Day by word of mouth, and sense they have an option to an open bar or a community agency. They soon get the feeling of the volunteers whose motto is "Be a friend; Meet a friend; Make a friend!"

Results. The guests have hot bread to smell and eat every Friday (some have not eaten for two or three days). They have a place to rest, meet, and share their lives. They know a caring community in the heart of a large city. They can receive crisis counseling. There is an information and referral service. Warmth and hope arise as many stay for a few minutes, or a few hours, or return two or three times in one day.

The volunteers have found meaning for their lives. They have discovered the meaning of local mission. There is therapy for arthritic hands and fingers. There is a sense of community fellowship and community involvement. Some have learned a new skill, the art of baking bread. All are convinced anybody can do it!

Future Plans. Leaders of the First Lutheran Church see the continuation of Bread Day as part of their ministry to the community. As they have discovered more of the needs of their complex guest clientele, they have sought the assistance of Lutheran Social Services of Southern California, San Diego Area Office. Bread Day is serving to lead this agency into an advocacy role in welfare issues. The hope is to broaden the base of service (volunteers) by creating a pan-Lutheran or pan-Christian organization to meet the varied needs of people who come to share hot bread.

The Cost. An average of 100 persons are served every Friday at a total cost per week of approximately $20.00.

For further information write to:

First Lutheran Church
1420 Third Avenue
San Diego, California 92101

Mid-Judicatory Program
Task Force on Older Adults
Synod of Southern California
United Presbyterian Church in the U.S.A.

A model of a mid-judicatory Task Force on Older Adults is included in this book because many local churches and synagogues look for help in ministries among older persons to larger groups in their organizational structures. It is there that initiation may best take place for consciousness-raising, training, coordination, evaluation, and general support. Such models are few. More need to be developed. The Task Force on Older Adults of the Synod of Southern California, United Presbyterian Church in the U.S.A. has been selected because of its potential, rather than because of its actual effectiveness.

SYNOD'S TASK FORCE IN OLDER ADULTS: Goals for 1972-1973.

The Synod's Task Force for Older Adults (TFOA) is to focus the concern of presbyteries and individual congregations on unmet needs of the community's elderly. This is to be accomplished by means of fact sheets and usable program ideas adapted to local circumstances. TFOA is authorized to develop a Task Force to serve each presbytery, and will assist local Sessions to develop a congregational Committee on Aging.

TFOA will encourage churches already providing direct service programs and invite others to bring their church's resources to bear on the elderly of their parish. The Task Force will arrange consultative resources to assist in developing local initiative. It will use its limited budget in setting up training conferences to make these years of its elderly parishioners as productive as it is capable of doing. Finally, the Synod TFOA is committed to an advocacy role and actively challenges the energies of each concerned congregation to support legislative action of particular benefit to the older American. Bi-monthly Older American Social Action Council Bulletins will be made available to requesting churches to keep them informed of legislative developments.

Suggestions for the Presbytery TFOA. Identify all groups and programs that the congregations are now sponsoring and report them to the Synod Task Force on Older Adults. Select an interested congregation or cluster of local churches to sponsor an action program such as those described below:

> Conduct a Retirement Preparation Program for persons aged 45 to 65.

> Provide a program on nutrition for the elderly, making full use of the new programs being funded by the federal government.

> Conduct a workshop on second career planning (coping with the work and leisure problem in retirement).

> Conduct a workshop on aging and organize a local Committee on Aging.

> Provide a counseling program that will meet the mental health needs of the aged.

> Organize a Senior Adult Multi-Service Center with direct services in the area of transportation, food service, housing, adult education, etc.

> Conduct in the local community a Conference on Aging.

Members of the Synod Task Force are available as speakers, conference leaders, and program implementors. They also have access to technical assistance for any of the programs listed above.

For further information write to:

Task Force on Older Adults
Synod of Southern California
United Presbyterian Church in the U.S.A.
1501 Wilshire Blvd.
Los Angeles, California 90017

Denominational Annual Retreats
"NIROGAS"
Nazarene International Retreats of Golden Agers

The Nazarene International Retreats of Golden Agers are denominationally-sponsored retreats for older persons. Because of their uniqueness and usefulness, they deserve a place in this book.

The idea for NIROGA was born in the mind of the Rev. Sam Stearman, Minister of Pastoral Care, First Church of the Nazarene, Bethany, Oklahoma, as he and another Nazarene pastor dreamed of a joint retreat for their two groups of older persons. With the help of Rev. Ponder Gilliland, Pastor of First Church of the Nazarene, Bethany, Oklahoma, the acronym NIROGA was created. At first, it meant National Invitational Retreat of Golden Agers, and the first NIROGA was held at Glorieta Baptist Conference Center (Southern Baptist), Glorieta, New Mexico, September 24-28, 1973. Four hundred fifty-seven older persons came from 27 states; from Alaska to Alabama; from California to Connecticut.

NIROGA II was held in 1974 at the same site with 1,040 in attendance from 34 states. The sponsorship was enlarged to include the entire Church of the Nazarene. The name was altered to Nazarene International Retreat of Golden Agers.

NIROGA III West was held in September, 1975, at Glorieta Conference Center with 920 present from 29 states, representing 35 of the 70 districts of the Church of the Nazarene. A number of guests from other denominations were also present. NIROGA East was held for the first time in Montreat, North Carolina, in October 1975, with a capacity 400 in attendance. More than 300 churches were represented in Niroga III. The year 1976 saw an expansion to three NIROGAS. In 1977, the number of NIROGAS was increased to five due to their popularity. Four were scheduled in the United States and one in Canada.

Nature and Purpose. Older persons throughout the Church of the Nazarene hear about NIROGAS from their local churches and in their denominational periodicals. Word of mouth carries the story far and wide. Throughout the year, plans are made to attend the annual conferences, with buses chartered to take the retreatants on an adventure that leads to fun, fellowship, inspiration, and renewal.

The purpose is to bring older persons together in beautiful settings where they can enjoy one another's company, good food, comfortable accommodations, workshops, arts and crafts, tours, games, and frequent worship. The retreats conclude with a magnificently planned and conducted banquet which makes every person feel an important part of the church, and of life. Each participant receives a specially designed medallion created for the NIROGA he or she attends.

The program is planned by the NIROGA Board, and is under the co-direction of Sam Stearman and Melvin Shrout. Worship services are held each day for the "Early Christians," 6:30 – 7:00 A.M.; "Later in the Day Saints," 8:30 – 9:30 A.M.; and in the evening at 8:00. Special music is part of all services except the early morning one. Afternoon bus tours are scheduled as extras for those who wish to visit scenic and historical spots, or shop in nearby areas. Arts and crafts are under the direction of younger church members. Prayer partners are assigned for the conference period. Retreat physicians are on call for emergency service. Shuttle buses are available to transport any person to and from the dining area.

The spirit of the NIROGAS is one of joy, peace, hope, love, and service to neighbor, born of a deep love for the Lord of Life. Many participants return to their churches and communities committeed to Senior Adult Ministries.

For further information write to:
The Rev. Sam Stearman
First Church of the Nazarene
6749 N.W. 39th Expressway
Bethany, Oklahoma 73008
　　or
The Rev. Melvin Shrout
Senior Adult Ministries
Church of the Nazarene
6401 The Paseo
Kansas City, Missouri 64131
　　or read
Senior Adult Ministries with Brother Sam, by Sam Stearman, Beacon Hill Press, Kansas City, Missouri, 1974.

REFERENCES

Peralta, Victorina. *Project: HEAD: Self-Help for the Elderly.* Department of Community Services on Aging, Catholic Social Services, Philadelphia, Pennsylvania: September 1974.

Stearman, Sam, *Senior Adult Ministries with Brother Sam.* Kansas City, Missouri: Beacon Hill Press, 1974.

6 Working At The Grass Roots

This chapter offers specific guidelines to enable leaders to work at the grass roots in developing and evaluating ministries among older persons. The reader is invited to consider the "How To" material presented which is the result of experiences gained in the Action/Investigation project of the Chatsworth Adult Center, Point Loma Community Presbyterian Church, San Diego, California. It is hoped that the step-by-step suggestions will stimulate action for beginning a ministry to, for, with, and of older persons in local congregations.

1. Begin Where You Are!

   The initiator may be a pastor, priest, rabbi, or lay person(s).

   Stop — Take time (it will probably be from some other priority).

   Look — Pay attention — look at older persons as if you have never seen them. Look with them at some common concern or need.

   Listen — Go where they are — homes, centers, parks,

gathering places, meetings, hospitals, nursing homes.

Aim — Try to see a bit of life as older persons see it.

2. Include Older Persons in your Life Space

Read — Newspapers, magazines, books that focus on older persons. Subscribe to *Dynamic Maturity* (AIM), *Modern Maturity* (AARP), or *The Gerontologist.*

Attend plays, watch television specials, movies; attend lectures related to aging and the aged.

Trust them — They have coped. They are for you. They can help. They have wisdom and experience.

Affirm them — Encourage them. Support them. Give them responsibility.

Touch them — Touching is talking. Sharing experiences, ideas, concerns is good therapy for all.

Respect them — Let them feel they are important to:

You	Church or Synagogue
Themselves	Community
God	Life

3. Ask yourself:

"What am I, what is our church or synagogue doing about older persons?"

Time spent: _____

_____

Activities: _____

_____

_____

What is good? _____

_____

What is poor? _____

_____

What am I (are we) feeling? _____

_____

4. Find Someone to Share your Concern
   A person   A committee
   A couple   A group
   A family

5. Involve a Committee or Official Board
   Report your concern. Suggest study of the matter. Seek concern and approval of the board. Indicate resources available, handbooks, etc. See "Tools for the Task" (Appendix).

6. Call Two Special Meetings of Interested People — One Week Apart
   a. First Meeting
      Get acquainted.
      Share common interests and concerns.
      Receive input from specialist(s), i.e., Area Agency on Aging, college professor, social worker, other community resource persons.
      Distribute *Claiming A Frontier: Ministry and Older People* for further study and action.
      Select chairperson, and two to eight other persons, mostly older, to form Steering Committee to choose Task Force on Older Adults.
      Let pastor, priest, rabbi, or his/her appointee serve as Advisor.
      Steering Committee should meet during the week before the next group meeting.
   b. Second Meeting
      Steering Committee reports recommendations for Task Force membership.
      Group selects Task Force on Older Adults.
      Show *The Second Spring of Samantha Muffin* (use *Study Guide for a Single Showing*).
      Review the congregation's present programs for older persons in light of Samantha Muffin's experience.
      Assign responsibility for developing ministries among older persons to Task Force.
      Task Force report to Official Board.

7. Work With the Task Force

Meet regularly: Weekly, bi-weekly, monthly, (More frequent meetings provide more input, stimulus, progress).

Materials: Continue use of *Claiming A Frontier: Ministry and Older People* and other books, handbooks, and manuals recommended in "resources."

The Second Spring of Samantha Muffin: Review one segment at each meeting (Use *Study Guide for Series of Programs.)*

Visit programs in community — ministries to, for, with, of older people. Evaluate.

Group sharing — at each meeting, share experiences, concerns, insights, information, feelings.

Records — Keep records of actions and progress.

8. Gather Information on Unmet Needs and Resources

Process includes:

Discovery — exploring and analyzing needs of the constituency.

Guiding — formation and integration of groups.

Helping — groups define and achieve goals.

Evaluating and Consolidating — group experience is put together through sharing.

Reference: *Older People and the Church,* Maves and Cedarleaf (1949).

Resources:

a. *Instructional Manual for the Older Adult Church Survey Project,* David L. Batzka (1974). This manual is designed to enable a local congregation Task Force to make important surveys:

Survey of members of congregation 55 years and older — questionnaire composed of 62 questions.

Community Social Service Survey containing 12 questions and guidelines.

Church Program Survey, including guidelines for conducting survey.

b. *Mission Action Group Guide: The Aging,* published by Woman's Missionary Union, Southern Baptist Church (1972).

Manual includes:

Personal preparation actions
Orientation actions
Survey actions
Planning actions
Process
Activities
In-service training action
Sharing actions
Resource list

c. *Senior Adult Utilization and Ministry Handbook* by Raymond A. Kader (1974).
Manual includes:
Perspective.
Utilizing the many talents of senior adults; survey forms most useful.
Ministering to active senior adults.
Ministering to shut-ins and nursing home senior adults.
Organizing small, middle size and large churches.

d. *Six Steps to Develop a Program for Older People,* compiled by Bella Jacobs (1972).
Manual includes:
Step One: Rationale for Program
Step Two: Form a Steering Committee
Step Three: Find a Sponsoring or Advisory Committee
Step Four: Group Structure
Step Five: First and Second open meetings
Step Six: Project in Operation

9. Consider Models of Programs
Resources: Use *Claiming A Frontier: Ministry and Older People,* also, *Aging Persons in the Community of Faith: A Guidebook for Churches and Synagogues on Ministry To, For and With the Aging,* by Donald F. Clingan (1975).
Review each model.
Consider which elements seem to meet apparent needs of your people in your situation.
List possible elements which you might include in a program for your congregation/community.
Dream of your potentials.

List names of persons who might help among your constituency.

Contact source of model(s) for further information.

10. Plan Your Program

Keep in mind that *you* are creating, revising programs for *your* situation. What works in another place *may* or *may not* be useful in yours. *Everyone* in this work is a *learner.* There is no right or wrong way.

Essential ingredients:

Needs and input of older persons themselves

Goal of *renewal* and *fulfillment* of older persons; not amusement, diversion, or killing of time.

Ministry *to, for, with,* and *of* older persons. Try for aspects of each of these in your program.

Be sure you know *why* you are doing *what* you are doing.

Evaluate results as you proceed (a mini-evaluation after each meeting in the early stages is often helpful).

Early course corrections may save grave mistakes. They also help in motivation and direction. They insure a valuable sense of "ownership" which is basic for long-range effectiveness.

Choose One Area of Focus

Pick the most urgent need discovered, or a genuine need you feel you can handle: i.e., Meals on Wheels, transportation, telephone reassurance, handyman service, educational classes, arts and crafts, Fellowship Programs, etc.

Involve Older People

Let it be theirs from the beginning. Use Senior Power.

Remember your situation is unique.

Build Program in Increments.

Add emphasis as you go, as needs and resources in persons and facilities emerge.

Consult specialists for direction.

Undergird your effort with personal and group prayer.

GENERAL CONSIDERATIONS

1. **Remember Relationships**
   Older people are a gold mine of experience, skills, and possibilities.
   Help them feel they belong to one another and to the group.
   Keep channels of participation open.

2. **Everybody Grow!**
   Look for signs of growth and involvement.
   Check "Twelve Rejuvenating Techniques" for guidelines of emphasis (Chapter 4).
   Be persistent and expectant.
   Progress will probably be like the growth of a snowball — slow at first, gaining in momentum, size, and effectiveness.
   Keep in mind the "signs of renewal and fulfillment" (Chapter 3).
   Enlarge scope to meet more needs of more people, and with more involvement.

3. **Key Factors**
   Spiritual concern for older persons as persons.
   Understanding.
   Patience.
   Flexibility.
   Involve older persons *always.*
   Support and encourage.
   Multiply leadership through participation and responsible delegation.
   Balance — There must be input if there is to be output.
   Motivate unceasingly.
   Feedback regularly to official board.
   Interpret program through word of mouth, and written communication in congregation and community.
   Do not let models scare you, especially if you are a beginner or in a small congregation.
   Programs of great usefulness can be in any size or type of congregation or community if wisely developed.
   Consider joining with another church or synagogue in your ministry among older persons.
   Use community resources.

SUMMARY

Begin where you are. Do your thing. Older people can experience renewal and fulfillment. They are able to help themselves with support from others. Stay with it. You will grow in effectiveness and do more. Show appreciation through recognition. The need is big. No one can do it all. Your contribution will help others. What you find and do may become more effective than anything any person or group has yet found and done.

There is no magic in this book. It calls for genuine interest and hard work. There are many resources in persons and material. Older people are the most important resource. Nobody can do for you and your church or synagogue what you and your congregation need to do.

BEGIN NOW!
CLAIM YOUR SHARE OF THE FRONTIER!!

REFERENCES

Aging Persons in the Community of Faith. A Congregational Guidebook for Churches and Synagogues on Ministry To, For, and With the Aging. Published for the Institute on Religion and Aging by the Indiana Commission on Aging and Aged, 1975.

Batzka, David L. *Instruction Manual for the Older Adult Church Survey Project.* The National Benevolent Association, the Division of Social and Health Services of the Christian Church (Disciples of Christ), Department of Service to Congregations, 1974.

Jacobs, Bella. "Six Steps to Develop a Program for Older People." The National Council on the Aging, Inc., Washington, D.C. 1972.

Kader, Raymond A. *Senior Adult Utilization and Ministry Handbook.* Clearwater, Florida: Kader Specialties, 1974.

Maves, Paul B. *Older People and the Church.* New York: Abingdon-Cokesbury Press, 1949.

Mission Action Group Guide: The Aging. Published by Woman's Missionary Union, Southern Baptist Church, 600 North 20th Street, Birmingham, Alabama 35203, 1972.

7

Reaping The Harvest

This chapter is written as a postscript, in anticipation of the reader's possible query, "But is it really worth it? What difference do you honestly feel it makes?"

I come to this task with a sense of gratitude and humility, for the frontier of ministry and the aging is one I had not expected to explore or seek to deal with in any special way. In the providence of God it has become a major and mounting concern in my ministry, and a means of looking at other aspects of my work as a pastor. What is shared here is but a small beginning. My hope is that it may encourage the reader to act.

A philosopher-friend tells the story of hiking alone on the mesas of New Mexico high country, when in the barrenness he came upon a single little flower which had pushed its way through the rock and was showing its face to the world. From his vantage point, the eons of geological ages were traceable in the cross-section of rock formation laid bare by the unending process of erosion. He stopped and pondered: "Little flower what are you doing out here alone? And what does your brief life have to do with the long eons of creation? How like you I am." Then his mood of meditation turned to prayer: "I hope you feel it is worth the blooming!"

I shall attempt to share a bit of the blooming I see, and begin with what may be called "general results." Reference was made to the unbroken continuation and growth of the Chatsworth Adult Center over the past three years. Average attendance has increased from six to over 100 each week. People are finding meaning in their participation. But who can say just why each person comes, and why most come every week? Is it not that something new has come into their lives — a place has come to have special meaning because of people — the people who gather to share themselves with one another? They come like settlers on the frontier to a camp meeting, bearing their sack lunches, books, handiwork, painting supplies, flowers, or simply wearing a smile of expectation or a frown of worry. They arrive in one's, two's and groups, knowing that wall-to-wall love awaits them as they enter the door and cross the threshold.

Something familiar will happen. A structured program of varied opportunities will unfold. And something new will occur. Out of the dynamics of the day, serendipitous happenings will gladden the heart, stimulate the mind, make the spirit dance, and the feet wish to follow! Affirmation unlocks imprisoned feelings, lifetime lessons seldom shared will be told. An experience of addition rather than subtraction will surprise and delight. Diminishment will subside, and new self-worth will emerge.

Someone will be ready to hear the story of the moment, or the recounting of the past, or the vision and plan for the future. If the ears of one person seem deaf today, others will hear. Listening will be accompanied with understanding, for those who have coped for so long have been in so many situations they seem to have a deep and quiet tryst with life! Those who have been in life a long time seem to know what is needed and how to help it happen.

Talents offered will not be turned down, but put to work. New skills will be learned. Creativity will blossom, and signs of it will be noted and appreciated by peers. Old friendships will deepen, and new ones will be born and may quickly grow. Telephone numbers will be exchanged, and so may prayers be shared for one another.

The Lord of Life who said, "I came that they may have life, and have it abundantly" (John 10:10b RSV), and, "Behold, I make all things new" (Revelation 21:5 RSV), seems to fulfill His promises in many forms: new relationships, new insights, new growth, new hope, new faith, new confidence, new concerns, new involvement, new courage, new commitments, new openness, new love, new joy!

By word of mouth the news spreads in the church and in the community through a kind of whispering campaign: "Try it, you'll like it!" The sound carries to the network of family and friends scattered across the nation and the world (several international visitors, friends, and family members have come and shared with pleasure).

Some will join the church and some will be married. Some will find new support for reaching into their lives and then reaching out to others, and vice versa. And if some should literally faint, peers trained in CPR are ready to respond until the ambulance arrives.

Little by little the fruit of the harvest is gathered. Many are beginning to believe about themselves and other older persons:

You have not had it!

You do need it!

You are worth it!

Something significant can be done!

Signs of renewal and fulfillment through maintenance, recovery and discovery are plainly evident. There is a perceptible rise in the good feeling of Senior Power, and a desire to reach out to those who are coming along behind with the double message, "Plan Now," and "To love is to grow!"

It is obvious that there is no retirement from aging. It is equally obvious that evidences of the harvest must be detectable in individual lives. No one knows just what the experience means for anyone else, but in the lives of a select few we can catch something of the first fruits of the harvest that may be traceable in others.

I like to think of our poet, a shy man, who came to San

Diego three years ago with his wife, hoping for improvement in his emotional and physical health. A long story is told in a few sentences. Through friendly interest of a member of the Center, they found us, and we found them. A sensitive man with a ream of poems on multiple subjects came to share his art, allowing us to take it apart, to follow, question, and augment his thought. Signs of new life crept into his aching spirit, and through his influence changes have been taking place in the group. So positive has his influence been that a paper was written by a member of the poetry group and read at the National Intra-Decade Conference on Spiritual Well-Being And The Elderly, April 12-14, 1977. He describes his own experience as "Renaissance."

One of the first persons to help our Center get underway has continued to invest herself with undiminished vigor. After a career as a social worker involved in overseeing the adoption of children, she has become a lover of older people with whom she identifies with unusual ability. "This is the most gratifying work I have ever done" is her witness.

A couple who have been in the church many years have found extended meaning for their lives as they have given able leadership to the development of the Center. Their labor of love turned into near full-time voluntary work in behalf of older persons. Their awareness of issues facing themselves and others has led them to use their energy and resources in bringing specific help to many persons seeking practical "survival" assistance in such matters as insurance, crime prevention, consumer fraud, nutrition, legal aid and tax assistance.

Into the life of the Center has come a man who at 83, following the death of his wife and sale of the family home, has chosen to transplant himself from the East Coast to the West Coast. Nearby live his sister and her husband. He came with two suitcases in which he packed his clothes and five pictures he has painted over the years. With a smile he is making his new home not only in a furnished apartment where he can hang his clothes and his pictures, but in the Center where he is finding new friends.

A quiet woman who spent a career of 40 years as an employee of a large store where she shared responsibility for the packing department, came to our community without friends. She wandered into the Center and began to absorb the spirit of sharing. After 40 years of packing, she is now unpacking her thoughts, feelings, hopes, and meanings. She is both loved and appreciated. She has been baptized and has become a part of the church as well as the Center, and is bringing others to share her wealth of newness!

The kitchen is filled every Tuesday with men who serve coffee, share experiences, and are ready to help members in any appropriate way. In a world where women have been the kitchen folk, there is always an element of surprise for those who come near and see the male kitchen-tenders.

A 90-year-old former teacher, who began her career in the midwest as a teen-age girl, and who has directed a private school for many decades, is still concerned for education and values. She comes each week to give and receive. Nearly blind, and burdened with other physical limitations, she nevertheless has a powerful influence for good by offering the rare gift of herself. The Scriptures speak of the patriarch of old: "By faith, Jacob . . . worshipped, leaning upon the top of his staff." (Hebrews 11:21 KJV.). So it is with her!

At last I come to myself. How does one, who like so many others has thought of himself as the younger member of groups, move with willingness into the ongoing stream of aging? Perhaps it is the positive modeling I have seen in older persons over the years. Perhaps it is the sensing that here is indeed a frontier with possibilities and promise. Perhaps it is the discovery that a little bit of love is enough for many to warm up to letting persons into the deep places of life. Perhaps it is the growing awareness of the untapped resources in older people so needed by our society. Perhaps it is all of these together that brought a single thought in the midst of worship one Sunday: "Older people make me feel at home in the world!" That thought has become both a benediction and an invocation – in that order. Perhaps it will serve in that way for you.

Early in the development of Chatsworth Adult Center, the Steering Committee, struggling to find its way, took time to reflect on its experiences and its feeling of the importance of ministry and older persons. I asked the small group to take crayons and draw pictures of their feelings. One man, a quiet intellectual type, complained that he could not draw. We told him he need not attempt it. But with that freedom he began and drew an unforgettable picture — a water pot sprinkling a flower! He and his wife moved before we really got under way, but the picture has remained as a promise. Now we are beginning to reap the harvest of good things which are coming from our attempts to claim the frontier of ministry and older people. To all we call, "Come and join us. There is room and need for everyone — for you!"

The frontier image has special meaning for the people of faith. The God of Israel has power to call individuals and a whole people to move out of safe places into adventure and risk. Abraham heard God's call with promise and left his ancestral home in Ur of the Chaldeans, moved by faith to pursue an unmarked trail to the land of Canaan. He became the chief patriarch of frontier people. Moses heard God's call and responded to lead his people from slavery in Egypt. They wandered 40 years in a wilderness and their leader did not make it. Still they moved onward until they entered and occupied the land. The prophets lived on the moral and spiritial frontier of love and justice, paying great prices for fidelity of witness and life.

After reciting heroic acts of faith and courage by an impressive list of the people of God, the writer of the Book of Hebrews calls for his readers to continue the frontier life, " . . . looking unto Jesus the pioneer and perfecter of our faith . . ." (Hebrews 12:2b, RSV). The Greek word *archēgos* is variously translated: "founder," "originator," "initiator" (as one who is founder of a city or family or philosophic school). An *archēgos* is one who blazes the trail for others to follow.

As a Christian I see Jesus Christ as the hero who surpasses all other heroes of faith, and as the *archēgos,* pioneer leader on every frontier of God's dealing with human life and destiny. He points out the frontiers and summons us to meet Him there, that together we may claim them for the enrichment of life under God. Those who seek to claim the frontier of ministry and older people may not only sense His presence but hear a new beatitude: "Blessed are those who claim the frontier of ministry and older people; for they shall discover the possibility of wholeness of life."

8 Tools For The Task

APPENDIX

Resources*

Effectiveness in beginning and expanding ministries among older persons may depend to a large degree on the awareness and availability of resources on a local, state, regional, or national scale. To assist those who wish such help, the following resources are suggested as "tools for the task."

1. Selected list of additional program models.

2. Total Community Service Organization Potential for Older Adult Programs.

---

*Portions of this section appear in Davis, R.H., "Resources in Gerontology," *Journal of Current Social Issues,* Vol. 14, No. 3, 1978; and in Clingan, D.C. *Aging Persons in the Community of Faith,* Institute on Religion and Aging: Indiana Commission on Aging and the Aged, 1975.

3. Selected list of National Organizations in the Field of Aging.

4. The Administration on Aging.

5. Selected list of Gerontology Centers.

6. Selected Bibliography (including books, published reports, handbooks and manuals, unpublished papers, audio-visuals).

I. ADDITIONAL PROGRAM MODELS

A. Programs conducted under religious auspices

Action — Senior Companions
Senior Adult Services
3445 30th Street
San Diego, California 92104

Fox Valley Older Adult Services
Box 125 or
120 South Main Street
Sandwich, Illinois 60548

John Knox Retirement Village
Lee's Summit,
Missouri 64063

P.A.L.
Immanuel Lutheran Church
1770 Brickell Avenue
Miami, Florida 33129

Project Compassion
The Board of Social Ministry and World Relief
The Lutheran Church — Missouri Synod
500 North Broadway
St. Louis, Missouri 63102

Project Ezra
197 East Broadway
New York, New York 10002

S.P.A. – Services Performed with Aging
Center City Churches for the Aging, Inc.
123 Ann Street
Hartford, Connecticut 06103

Saint Mary's Extended Care Center
2512 Seventh Street South
Minneapolis, Minnesota 55406

Salvation Army
Phoenix Corps
618 North Third Avenue
Phoenix, Arizona 85003

School of Continuing Education
St. Luke's United Methodist Church
1506 North Harvey Street
Oklahoma City, Oklahoma 73103

Seagull Volunteer Program
Protestant Social Services
3637 N.E. First Avenue
Miami, Florida 33137

Senior Activities Centers
540 21st Street
Oakland, California 94612

Senior Center
Brighton Reformed Church
805 Blossom Road
Rochester, New York 14610

Senior Talent Employment Poor (S.T.E.P.)
Family Services
303 South Wright
Champaign, Illinois 61820

Services to Seniors
San Francisco Council of Churches;
Adult Division
San Francisco Community College District
Pacific Heights Community College Education Center
31 Gough Street
San Francisco, CA 94103

Telecare Ministry
Hanover Avenue Christian Church
Robert W. Maphis, Minister
1723 Hanover Avenue
Richmond, Virginia 23220

Two Day Care Centers:
Our Lady of Lourdes
2400 Napoleon Avenue 70115
          and
Christopher Inn
2110 Royal
New Orleans, Louisiana 70116

Westside Ecumenical Ministry to the Elderly
2095 Broadway
New York, NY 10025

B. **Programs conducted under secular auspices**

Active Clevelanders Today
11720 Lorain Avenue
Cleveland, Ohio 44111

California Legislative Council on Older Americans
330 Ellis Street
San Francisco, California 94102

Emeritus College
College of Marin County
Kentfield, California 94904

Gray Panthers
3700 Chestnut Street
Philadelphia, Pennsylvania 19104

Joseph B. Knowles Center
1801 Broadway
Nashville, Tennessee 37203

Kiwanis, International
101 East Erie Street
Chicago, Illinois 60611

Minneapolis Age and Opportunity Center, Inc.
1801 Nicollet Avenue
Minneapolis, Minnesota 55403

Northeast New Jersey Community Action Union Project
116 North Oraton Parkway
East Orange, New Jersey 07017

North Shore Senior Center
620 Lincoln Avenue
Winnetka, Illinois 60093

Retired Senior Volunteer Program (RSVP)
806 Connecticut Avenue, N.W.
Washington, D.C. 20525

Senior Citizens' Alliance of Greater Philadelphia
1213 Race Street
Philadelphia, Pennsylvania 19107

II. TOTAL COMMUNITY SERVICE ORGANIZATION POTENTIAL FOR OLDER ADULT PROGRAMS

Economic Organizations
Corporations
Chamber of Commerce
Vocational Groups
    Unions
    Retail Merchants Association
    Farmers Association
    Boards of Banks, Corporations
    Professional Associations

Government Organizations
Federal Departments & Agencies
 (Local offices: General Services Administration, Equal
 Employment Opportunity Commission, Department of
 Health, Education and Welfare, etc.)
State Departments and Agencies
 (Local offices: Bureau of Vocational Rehabilitation,
 Health Department, Welfare Department, etc.)
County Departments and Agencies
 (Local offices: Aid for the Aged, Cooperative Exten-
 sion, Welfare Department, etc.)
Community Departments and Agencies
 (Recreation Department, Welfare Department, Health
 Department, Housing Division, Board of Education,
 etc.)

Education Organizations
Better School Groups
Parent-Teacher Organizations
Adult Education Groups

Religious Organizations
Churches and Synagogues
Groups associated with churches and synagogues
Ecumenical organizations, commissions
Clergy associations
Laymen associations
Primarily religious (Bible Study Groups, Worship Groups)
Other (Clubs, Teams, Social Groups)

Cultural, Fraternal and Recreational Organizations
Concert societies
Study and forum groups
Art societies
Dramatic groups
Literary societies
Nationality group fraternal association
Occupation-oriented fraternal ass'ns (Police leagues)
Other fraternities, lodges, granges, secret societies
Athletic teams
Athletic clubs

Hobby clubs
Social enjoyment groups
Groups serving one particular minority

Civic Organizations
Service Clubs
Good government leagues
Patriotic and veterans associations
Taxpayers associations
Political party organizations
Neighborhood planning associations
Real estate associations
Housing associations

Health and Welfare Organizations
Charitable organizations
Religious charitable organizations
Boards of social agencies
Welfare or humane associations
Child welfare organizations
Youth organizations
Federations of professional workers
Organizations of particular diseases (heart, cancer, arthritis)
General community health groups
Safety council

Community and Planning Organizations
United community service organizations
Chests, united funds, councils
Community action agencies (poverty)
Community planning associations
Coordinating committees
Federations of clubs
Other intergroup agencies or organizations

Specific Community Resources for Older Adult Programs
Look in your local "Yellow Pages" under Social Service
Organizations for addresses and telephone numbers of
such organizations as:
AFL-CIO Community Service
ACTION (R.S.V.P.)

Area Agencies on Aging
Catholic Social Service
Community Action Program
Community Service Council
Community Mental Health Agency
Community College
Council of Churches
Family Service Association
Foster Grandparent Program
Home Health Care Agency
Homemaker Service
Information & Referral Service
Jewish Family Service
Legal Service Organization
Meals on Wheels
Title VII Nutrition Program
Park and Recreation Department
Public Housing Authority
Public Library
Salvation Army
Senior Citizens Center
Settlement Center
Social Security Administration
UAW Community Service
University
Urban League
Visiting Nurses Association
YMCA and YWCA

III. NATIONAL ORGANIZATIONS

Action for Independent Maturity (AIM)
1909 K St., N.W.
Washington, D.C. 20049

Adult Education Association of the U.S.A.
810 18th St., N.W.
Washington, D.C. 20006

Altrusa International, Inc.
332 South Michigan Ave.
Chicago, Ill. 60604

American Aging Association
University of Nebraska Medical Center
Omaha, Nebr. 68105

American Association of Homes for the Aging
1050 17th St., N.W.
Washington, D.C. 20036

American Association of Retired Persons
1909 K St., N.W.
Washington, D.C. 20049

American Foundation for the Blind, Inc.
15 West 16th St.
New York, N.Y. 10011

American Geriatrics Society
10 Columbus Circle
New York, N.Y. 10019

American Health Care Association
2500 15th St., N.W.
Washington, D.C. 20015

American Legion
700 N. Pennsylvania St.
Indianapolis, Ind. 46208

Committee on Retired Workers,
United Steelworkers of America
1500 Commonwealth Ave.
Pittsburgh, Pa. 15222

Gerontological Society
1 Dupont Circle
Washington, D.C. 20036

Gray Panthers
3700 Chestnut Street
Philadelphia, PA 19104

The Institute on Ministry and the Elderly
Kansas Newman College
3100 McCormick Avenue
Wichita, Kansas 27213

Institute for Retired Professionals
The New School for Social Research
60 West 12th St.
New York, N.Y. 10011

International Federation on Aging
1909 K St., N.W.
Washington, D.C. 20049

International Senior Citizens Association, Inc.
11753 Wilshire Blvd.
Los Angeles, Calif. 90025

Jewish Association for Services for the Aged
222 Park Ave. South
New York, N.Y. 10003

Kiwanis International
101 East Erie St.
Chicago, Ill. 60611

National Alliance of Senior Citizens
Box 40031
Washington, D.C. 20016

National Association of Jewish Homes for the Aged
2525 Centerville Rd.
Dallas, Texas 75228

National Federation of Grandmother Clubs of America
203 North Wabash Ave.
Chicago, Ill. 60601

National Association of Retired Federal Employees
1533 New Hampshire Ave., N.W.
Washington, D.C. 20036

National Caucus on the Black Aged
1730 M St., N.W.
Washington, D.C. 20036

National Center for Voluntary Action
1785 Massachusetts Ave., N.W.
Washington, D.C. 20036

National Council on the Aging, Inc.
1828 L St., N.W., Suite 504
Washington, D.C. 20036

National Council for Homemaker-Home Health Aide Services
67 Irving Place
New York, N.Y. 10003

National Council of Senior Citizens
1511 K St., N.W., Rm. 202
Washington, D.C. 20005

National Geriatrics Society, Inc.
212 West Wisconsin Ave.
Milwaukee, Wis. 53203

National Interfaith Coalition on Aging, Inc.
P.O. Box 1986
Indianapolis, Ind. 46206

National Retired Teachers Association
1909 K St., N.W.
Washington, D.C. 20049

National Tenants Organization
1346 Connecticut Ave., N.W.
Washington, D.C. 20036

Oliver Wendell Holmes Association
381 Park Ave. South
New York, N.Y. 10016
(This group is interested in the expansion of the intellectual horizons of older people.)

Volunteers of America
340 West 85th St.
New York, N.Y. 10024

IV. U. S. ADMINISTRATION ON AGING
330 C. St., S.W.
HEW South
Washington, D.C. 20201

Regional Offices of the Administration on Aging

Region I (Conn., Maine, Mass., N.H., R.I., Vt.)
J. F. Kennedy Federal Bldg.
Government Center, Room 2007
Boston, Mass. 02203

Region II (N.J., N.Y., Puerto Rico, Virgin Islands)
26 Federal Plaza, Rm. 4106
Broadway and Lafayette St.
New York, N.Y. 10007

Region III (Del., D.C., Md., Pa., Va., W. Va.)
P.O. Box 13716
3535 Market St., 5th Fl.
Philadelphia, Pa. 19101

Region IV (Ala., Fla., Ga., Ky., Miss., N.C., S.C., Tenn.)
50 Seventh St., N.E., Rm. 326
Atlanta, Ga. 30323

Region V (Ill., In., Mich., Minn., Ohio, Wis.)
300 S. Wacker Dr., 29th Fl.
Chicago, Ill. 60606

Region VI (Ark., La., N. Mex., Okla., Tex.)
Federal Building
1114 Commerce St.
Dallas, Texas 75202

Region VII (Iowa, Kans., Mo., Nebr.)
601 East 12th St.
Kansas City, Mo. 64106

Region VIII (Colo., Mont., N. Dak., S. Dak., Utah, Wyo.)
Federal Office Bldg., Rm. 9017
19th and Stout Sts.
Denver, Colo. 80202

Region IX (Ariz., Calif., Hawaii, Nev., Samoa, Guam, T.T.)
Federal Office Bldg., Rm. 204
50 Fulton St.
San Francisco, Calif. 94102

Region X (Alaska, Idaho, Oreg., Wash.)
1319 2nd Ave., Mezzanine (Arcade Plaza)
Seattle, Wash. 98101

State

Each state has its Department, Office, or Commission on Aging. The address is usually at the state capital. In addition, each state has numbers of local Area Agencies on Aging. Addresses can be obtained from state offices.

V. GERONTOLOGY CENTERS IN EDUCATIONAL INSTITUTIONS*

Boston University
Gerontology Center
Boston, Mass. 02215

Brandeis University
Florence Heller School
Waltham, Mass. 02154

Chicago, University of
Adult Development and Aging Program
Chicago, Ill. 60637

---

*Note: This list is by no means complete. It is representative and attempts to cite major programs. *The National Directory of Educational Programs in Gerontology* (DHEW publication, Supt. of Documents, U.S. Govt. Printing Office, Washington, D.C. 20402, $9.35) has information on gerontology programs of 2,275 colleges and universities.

Duke University
Center for the Study of Aging and Human Development
Durham, N.C. 27710

Florida, University of
Center for Gerontological Studies
Gainesville, Florida 32611

Michigan, University of
Institute of Gerontology
Ann Arbor, Mich. 48109

North Texas State University
Center for Studies on Aging
Denton, Tex. 76203

Pennsylvania State University
Gerontology Center
University Park, Penna. 16802

South Florida, University of
Institute on Aging
Tampa, Florida 33620

Southern California, University of
Andrus Gerontology Center
Los Angeles, Ca. 90007

Syracuse, University of
All University Gerontology Center
Syracuse, N.Y. 13210

VI. SELECTED BIBLIOGRAPHY

A. Books

Atchley, Robert C. *The Social Forces in Later Life: An Introduction to Social Gerontology.* Belmont, California: Wadsworth, 1972.

Buckley, Joseph C. *The Retirement Handbook.* New York: Harper and Row, 1971.

Butler, Robert N., M.D. *Why Survive? Being Old in America.* New York: Harper and Row, 1975.

Comfort, Alex, *A Good Age.* New York: Crown Publishers, Inc., 1976.

Crippen, Dorothy, *et al.,* eds. *The Wisdom of Ethel Percy Andrus.* Long Beach, California: NRTA/ AARP, 1968.

Culver, Elsie T. *New Church Programs with the Aging.* New York: Association Press, 1961.

Davis, Richard H., ed. *Aging: Prospects and Issues.* Ethel Percy Andrus Gerontology Center, University of Southern California, 1976.

Duder, Edwin F. *Time is a Gypsy.* Canton, Connecticut: The Caywood Publishing Co., 1963.

Galton, Lawrence. *Don't Give Up on an Aging Parent.* New York: Crown Publishers, Inc., 1975.

Hiltner, Seward, ed. *Toward a Theology of Aging.* A special issue of Pastoral Psychology, New York Human Sciences Press, 1975.

Howe, Reuel L. *How to Stay Younger While Growing Older.* Waco, Texas: Word Books, 1974.

Hunter, Woodrow W. *Preparation for Retirement.* Institute of Gerontology, University of Michigan, Wayne State University, Ann Arbor, Michigan, 1973.

Maves, Paul B., and Cedarleaf, J. Lennart. *Older People and the Church.* New York: Abingdon-Cokesbury Press, 1949.

Moberg, David O., and Gray, Robert M. *The Church and the Older Person.* Grand Rapids, Michigan: William B. Eerdmans, 1962.

Morgan, John H. *Ministering to the Elderly: Perspectives and Opportunities.* Institute on Ministry and the Elderly, Wichita, Kansas, 1977.

Neugarten, Bernice L. *Personality in Middle Life and Late Life.* New York: Atherton Press, 1964.

Nouwen, Henri J.M. and Gaffney, Walter J. *Aging.* Garden City, New York: Doubleday and Co., Inc., 1974.

Percy, Charles H., Senator. *Growing Old in the Country of the Young.* New York: McGraw-Hill Co., 1974.

Robb, Thomas Bradley. *The Bonus Years.* Valley Forge, Pennsylvania: Judson Press, 1968.

Schuckman, Terry. *Aging is Not for Sissies.* Philadelphia: Westminister Press, 1975.

Smith, Bert K. *Aging in America.* Boston: Beacon Press, 1973.

Stearman, Sam. *Senior Adult Ministries with Brother Sam.* Kansas City, Missouri: Beacon Hill Press, 1974.

Tournier, Paul. *Learn to Grow Old.* New York: Harper and Row, 1971.

B. Published Reports

A Center Report: Life Enrichment Ministry with the Elderly. Center for Parish Development, 320 East School Avenue, Naperville, Illinois, 60540. April 1973.

On Being Alone: AIM's Guide for Widowed Persons. James A. Peterson. Action for Independent Maturity, 1909 K Street, N.W., Washington, D.C. 20006

Spiritual Well-Being. Background, David O. Moberg, Ph.D., White House Conference on Aging, Washington, D.C. 20201.

The Aging and the United Presbyterian Church in the U.S.A. Charles G. Chakerian, ed. New York: Division of Health and Welfare, Board of National Missions, 1964.

The Church and the Aging. A Survey Report on Ministers of the United Presbyterian Church in the U.S.A., April 1967.

The Church and the Aging. Position Paper. Austin, Texas: Texas Conference on Churches, June 1974.

The Rights and Responsibilities of Older Persons. Policy Statement and Recommendations Adopted by the 185th General Assembly of the U.P.C.U.S.A. Lancaster, Pennsylvania: Program Agency of U.P.C.U.S.A. and the Board of Christian Education of the Presbyterian Church in the United States, October 1973.

Toward a National Policy on Aging — 1971 White House Conference on Aging, Final Report. Vol. 1 and Vol. 2, November 28 — December 2, 1971.

C. Handbooks and Manuals

A Comprehensive Program for the Elderly in Rural Areas. Suzannah Chandler. The National Council on the Aging, Inc., for the Community Action Program, Office of Economic Opportunity

Aging Persons in the Community of Faith. A Congregational Guidebook for Churches and Synagogues on Ministry to, for and with the Aging, Donald F. Clingan. Published for the Institute on Religion and Aging by the Indiana Commission on Aging and Aged, 1975.

Batzka, David L. *Instruction Manual for the Older Adult Church Survey Project.* The National Benevolent Association, the Division of Social and Health Services of the Christian Church (Disciples of Christ), Department of Service to Congregations, 1974.

Continuous Choices: A Comprehensive Handbook of Programs for Work with Older Adults. National Council of Jewish Women, Inc., 1975.

Guidelines for a Telephone Reassurance Service. Virginia Robers, Institute of Gerontology, University of Michigan-Wayne State University, Ann Arbor, Michigan: Missouri Office of Aging, Department of Community Affairs, 1969.

How to Organize a Senior Center. National Institute of Senior Centers, 1828 L Street, N.W., Washington, D.C. 20036.

How to Organize an AARP Chapter. A Guide for the State Director and the Steering Committee. AARP, Washington, D.C. January 1973.

Jacobs, Bella. *Involving Men: A Challenge for Senior Centers.* National Council on the Aging, Inc. March 1974.

Jacobs, Bella. "Six Steps to Develop a Program for Older People," The National Council on the Aging, Inc., Washington, D.C. 1972.

Leanse, Joyce and Jacobs, Bella. *Working With Older People.* The National Council on the Aging, Inc., Washington, D.C. October 1972.

Maxwell, Jean M. *Centers for Older People: Guide for Programs and Facilities.* The National Council on the Aging, Inc., 1962, Reprint 1973.

Mission Action Group Guide: The Aging. Published by Woman's Missionary Union, 600 North Twentieth Street, Birmingham, Alabama 35204. 1972.

Project: HEAD. Victorina Peralta, Department of Community Services on Aging, Catholic Social Services, Philadelphia, Pennsylvania. Revised Edition, 5th Printing, September 1974.

Senior Adult Utilization and Ministry Handbook. Raymond A. Kader, Kader Specialties Publisher, Clearwater, Florida, 1974.

Stough, Ada Barnett. *Brighter Vistas: Church Programs for Older Adults.* Case Study No. 18, U.S. Department of Health, Education and Welfare, Administration on Aging, Washington, D.C. 1965.

The Multi-Purpose Senior Center. A Model Community Action Program prepared by the National Council on the Aging, Inc., Washington, D.C., for the Office of Economic Opportunity. Revised, June 1972.

Spiritual Well-Being. Report of Special Study Consultation to develop a Definition and Interpretation of Spiritual Well-being as it may be applicable to Aging and the Religious Sector, NICA. March 27, 1975.

D. Audio-Visuals

About Aging: A Catalog of Films. Compiled by: Mildred V. Allyn, Project Editor. Andrus Gerontology Center, University of Southern California, Los Angeles, California 90007.

A Matter of Indifference. A critique of our society's ambivalence toward its aged. 16mm — b/w — 50 minutes. Order from Phoenix Films, Inc., 743 Alexander Road, Princeton, New Jersey 08540.

Housing Options for Older People. Created to serve as a basis of discussion for older persons and their families. It does not make judgements, and it does not deal with nursing homes. 16mm – color – 28 minutes. Order from ETV Center, MVR Hall, Cornell University, Ithaca, New York 14935.

Journey's End. Planning for the end of life (estate, funeral, etc.) 16mm – color – 27 minutes. Available on loan from NRTA/AARP Regional Offices, or write to NRTA/AARP Public Relations, 1909 "K" Street, N.W. Washington, D.C. 20049, or University of Southern California, Film Distribution Center, Division of Cinema, University Park, Los Angeles, California 90007.

Making Retirement Constructive. An effective, provocative interview with Layona Glenn, still dynamically alive at 102! 16mm – b/w – 15 minutes. Order from Institute of Lifetime Learning, AARP, 1225 Connecticut Ave. N.W., Washington, D.C. 20036.

May Your Years Be Long. Film presents points of view and philosophy of several leading gerontologists about housing, pre-retirement planning, etc. 16mm – b/w – 30 minutes. Order from Institute of Lifetime Learning, AARP, 1225 Connecticut Ave. N.W., Washington, D.C. 20036.

Nobody Ever Died of Old Age. Drawn from the best-selling book of the same title by Sharon Curtin. Recreates a series of her real-life experiences and vivid perceptions of what it's like to be old in America today. 16mm – color.

Old, Black and Alive! Seven elderly blacks share their insight, faith, and strength in a compelling documentary of aging. 16mm – color – sound. Order from The New Film Company, Inc., 3331 Newbury St., Boston, MA 02115.

Old Fashioned Woman. The perspective of age. Assumption by older persons of an active role in providing an image or model for the young.

(Generations). A 16mm – 40 minutes – color. Order from Films, Inc., 1144 Wilmette Avenue, Wilmette, Ill. 60091.

Other People Make Me Feel Old. An instrument for raising consciousness about the problems associated with aging. Three parts. A 16mm – 31 minutes – color. Order from The Learning Resources Center, University of Oklahoma Health Sciences Center, P.O. Box 26901, Oklahoma City, OK 73190.

Peege. A family visits a grandmother in a nursing home at Christmas. She is blind and has lost some of her mental faculties. 16mm – color – 28 minutes. Order from Phoenix Films, Inc., 743 Alexander Road, Princeton, New Jersey 08540.

That's What Living's About. A lively but philosophical look at leisure – what it means, how it affects our lives now, and how it may affect them in the future. 16mm – color – 18 minutes. Order from University of California Extension Media Center, Berkeley, CA 94720.

The Second Spring of Samantha Muffin. An eighty-two year old mouse is remotivated by the Twelve Rejuvenating Techniques. 145 frame filmstrip and cassette, script and study guide. 32½ minutes. Cost $10.00. Order from United Presbyterian Health, Education and Welfare Association, 475 Riverside Drive, New York, NY 10027.

The Third Age: The New Generation. Film on the creative contribution older persons can and should be prepared to give to society through the support of the church/synagogue. For information on rental, write Audio Visual Library, P.O. Box 1986, Indianapolis, IN 46206.

Volunteer to Live! A 30 minute color sound 16mm film documentary of the inter-faith ministry with the aging at Shepherd's Center, Kansas City, Missouri. For rental order form: Audio-Visual Library, P.O. Box 1986, Indianapolis, Indiana 46206.

We've Come of Age. Recounts the accomplishments of the generation now "old" and exhorts them to unite for their common good. 16mm — color — 12 minutes. Order from National Council of Senior Citizens, Film Section, 1511 K St. N.W., Washington, D.C. 20005.

INDEX

About the Author

Robert W. McClellan is a native of Los Angeles. He was a student (1935-1939) of Dr. Ethel Percy Andrus, founder of AARP/NRTA, when she was a principal of Abraham Lincoln High School, and he later graduated from the University of California at Los Angeles. (B.A.) He was awarded a Bachelor of Divinity degree by Princeton Seminary and a Doctor of Ministry degree by San Francisco Theological Seminary. He holds an honorary Doctor of Divinity degree from Occidental College in Los Angeles.

Dr. McClellan has served churches in the United Presbyterian Church in the U.S.A. for more than thirty years, including pastorates as Head of Staff in Philadelphia, Pa., La Jolla, Ca., Kailua, Ha., and San Marino, Ca. He is currently an Associate Pastor of the Point Loma Community Presbyterian Church in San Diego, Ca., where he has led in the formation and development of Chatsworth Adult Center described in this book.

He is married to the former Mildred Louise Walker, and is father of two daughters and a grandfather twice.